CW00417345

AWARENESS ITSELF

Being Aware of Awareness Itself Is the Key

AWARENESS ITSELF

Being Aware of Awareness Itself Is the Key

PAUL F. GORMAN

Edited by M.L.

 VINE PRESS
NAPA, CALIFORNIA

Other Books by Paul F. Gorman

Releasing the Universe Within

The Great Need

I Am (A Meditation)

I Am Now (A Meditation)

One

The Miracle Self

The Giving Self

Healing of The Body

The Way of Awakening

Satisfied With God Alone

Bringing Forth The Presence of God

Anyone Can Demonstrate Infinity

The Impersonal Self

The Inner Sanctuary

The Seven Spiritual Steps To Solving Any Problem

Opening The Windows of Heaven

Only God Is

The Fully Manifest Presence

That Which You Seek

Many free writings are available at www.miracleself.com

Rise in conscious awareness—this is the entire secret.

As conscious awareness rises, detaching from and
leaving behind belief, ever greater degrees of heaven
become visible through the unconditioned mind.

"As in heaven so on earth."

The earth and all its people, things and conditions
are witnessed unconditioned, whole and harmonious,
love and union of all emerging through the dissipating
fog of belief.

Indeed, "As in heaven so on earth" emerges as the one reality.
The false bondage of material sense is dispelled, and the
unconditioned experience of man, earth and universe
is experienced harmonious, peaceful and free, in love.

Paul F. Gorman

Awareness Itself: Being Aware of Awareness Itself Is the Key

Copyright © 2018 by Paul F. Gorman

All rights reserved. No part of this book may be reproduced or transmitted in any form without the express permission in writing from the publisher, except by a reviewer who may quote brief passages for review purposes.

FIRST PAPERBACK EDITION 2018

ISBN-13: 978-1-7322122-8-2

ISBN-10: 1-7322122-8-7

Published by Vine Press, Napa, California

Set in Garamond ATF 10.5/13

Available worldwide from Amazon and all other online and traditional book stores

www.miracleself.com

CONTENTS

INTRODUCTION

Eight years ago, I posted a short essay on the Miracle Self website titled *Awareness Itself: Being Aware of Awareness Itself Is the Key*. It has consistently been among the top twelve (of over 3600) of the site's pages ever since.

Awareness Itself is *I (God)*, the true identity of being, the substance, form, and activity of all that we are, inclusive of all that constitutes the universe we are aware *of*. Awareness Itself is the one, all-of-all, inner and outer.

What appears to be "three" — *we*, that which we are aware *of*, and that which we are aware *with* — is one and the same existence, presence, form, and experience.

Awareness Itself has been called and is synonymous with *God, Consciousness, Spirit, Truth, Infinity, Omnipresence, Omniscience, Omnipotence, Presence, I, I am,* and *I am that.* Perhaps *Awareness Itself* registers most deeply for many.

Becoming consistently aware of, and living as Awareness Itself is the key to witnessing the infinity of good within and without. As we gently yet consistently remain aware of Awareness Itself, the good of unconditioned experience becomes our reality.

Being aware of Awareness Itself is the key.

As we become more aware of the infinity of our awareness instead of believing the appearing limits, lacks and discords of finite sense, we discover vitality and limitlessness opening as our experience. It requires only a subtle shift in awareness and immersion. This shift, gently yet faithfully maintained each day, is our access to the infinity of good.

I have watched students struggle with true awareness for years. Now, the seasoned guidance and practice given in this book enable the individual to lift awareness from the finiteness of personal and material limit to that of Awareness Itself — the immediacy and boundlessness of life.

As we even touch the hem of Awareness Itself, the doors of infinity and harmony open. The fog of false sense dissipates to reveal true being, body and world, and we begin to witness harmony and plenty where discord and lack appeared to be.

Let us be assured that none of God, good, is absent or unavailable to immediate, tangible experience. Good is not far away but is "closer than breathing, and nearer than hands and feet". ("The Higher Pantheism," Lord Alfred Tennyson) However, we have to open our awareness to that which true good *is* in order to experience it.

This minute, the good you sense as most needed in your life exists right where you are in fully manifested, demonstrated and visible form, no matter what the need appears to be. As quickly as material sense is lifted into Awareness Itself, sensed discord, disease, lack and limitation dissolve, and harmony emerges.

When a Need Is Pressing

Over the ten years of teaching the Miracle Self, I have watched even long-term truth students continue to struggle to let go of *things* (as we all do, to begin with) and lift their awareness into the one real presence, substance, form and experience of Awareness Itself.

God (fulfillment, true identity) can only do *for us* what it can do *through us*. If true identity is not understood, it cannot *get through* our belief in its absence. No matter how consistently we study, pray, meditate and sit in silence, we are unable to see and to have the objective forms of true good in real and practical experience. "Know the truth, and the truth will make you free." We have to know truth before its reality and visibility become tangible to sense.

Practicing the Presence of Awareness Itself

Working closely with hundreds of students over these years, I have found that practicing the presence of Awareness Itself evidences marvelous fruits for those who give it their daily devotion.

The idea of attaining "God consciousness" is difficult for many, but changing the terminology frees us from deeply imbedded beliefs in separation and difference from God.

When we awaken to our true identity and withdraw our attention, our sense of need, and our effort from the people and things of outer sense, maintaining our awareness of Awareness Itself, we discover the miracles of health, abundance, harmony, and fulfillment of purpose are freely ours. Awareness Itself felt within is the "cause" of its outer image and likeness being evident, and harmony prevails.

Acts of Awareness

As you read on now, realize this (from a recent *Awareness Itself* class):

> Here is the great secret. If you can hear it, if it registers within you now, your life and circumstances will transform almost instantly and forever.

Because all is Awareness Itself, it is not by mental might, physical effort or material manipulation but by *acts of awareness* that we discover our true identity and the harmonies of life. It is by acts of awareness that truth becomes visible, tangible, real; that healing takes place, that prosperity takes place; that the multiplication of loaves and fishes, of dollars, of business success, of opportunity, of love, of spiritual realization comes about in individual experience.

P.F.G

April 21st, 2018

Awareness
Itself

Being Aware of Awareness Itself Is the Key

CHAPTER ONE

Awareness Itself

Awareness Itself is what you are. Awareness Itself is what every person, thing, and condition is. Awareness Itself is what the infinity of your universe constitutes. Awareness Itself is what has been called God, Consciousness, *I* or *I Am,* and other synonyms.

This minute, you are and have all that Awareness Itself is and has. The collective belief you hold about it and your personal sense of it finitize your awareness but never your reality. You see only a minuscule fraction of a fraction of that which you truly are and have, that which is the infinity of good filling your mind, body, and world.

Feel Awareness

Begin to feel the presence of (experience) your awareness. You do not have to think about or do anything with it. Simply *feel* — *experience* — your awareness "happening."

You do not have to understand anything about it. Simply
feel it happening.

Relax in it. Truly let go in it. Yield your sense of awareness to Awareness Itself. Let Awareness Itself take over.
Begin to feel the deep peace welling up, filling you.

Even though it may seem to be contained within your
physical sense, it is not. It fills your universe. It is inside you
and outside you. It is your all-good, your truth, your safety,
your protection and your protec*tor* itself. It is what has been
called spirit and truth, the finished kingdom of all.

The authority for what we are to hear will unfold
through the pages of this book so that you have real and
strong certainty about the truth, about the unconditional
good that is yours at every moment and is instantly available
to your apprehension, to your experience at every moment.
For right now, though, realize (or begin to be open to) the
fact that the awareness that you feel *is itself* your infinite
good, fully formed and visible throughout every aspect of
your life. As you begin to awaken to it you will quickly experience its harmonies and joys.

This pure awareness is and sees you — your truth, the you
you truly are, the mind you truly are and have, the body you
truly have, the world you truly experience — as its perfection,
wholeness, completeness, eternity, invariability this instant.

We are going to discover how to lift into that state of
non-self (non-personal self) in order that awareness sees *for
us, is* for us, *is being* everything we are being *for us,* is aware of
everything we are aware of *for us* — not as we believe it is,
but as it truly is, right here on earth.

We are not speaking of an ethereal awareness that re-
moves us from our immediate, three-dimensional, so-called
"human, worldly, physical, material" experience. There is
no such different existence. This, right here where you are,
is the one kingdom. "The place upon which you stand is

holy ground." That statement is being uttered to each and every one of us, not just a holy man of three thousand years ago. You are the holy woman and man, and the place whereon you stand is holy ground; the place of your existence this day is holy ground, is God. Whatever seems to be going on, good or bad, in your life is not in itself what is actually happening, what is actually present where that situation appears to be. What is happening is *truth*. The only presence is truth (God, good); the only person, thing, activity, amount and place is unconditional truth.

As we learn to drop our personal sense of awareness and lift into the state in which Awareness Itself sees, hears, tastes, touches, smells and thinks for us — *as* individual us — then we have the tangible, visible reality of good or God.

Realize, know, accept that this Awareness Itself (not our sense of it, but the Awareness Itself we experience) is the kingdom of God (the kingdom of good) fully formed, fully visible, fully manifested, fully demonstrated, fully real, fully practical, as the entirety of you, the whole universe of you, every grain of you, every aspect of your experience, your life — every, *every* aspect; every being, thing, cell, atom; every form, every amount, every activity, every place.

It is all the kingdom of truth, the kingdom of God. Why is that true? Because the kingdom of God is the only kingdom. The being that is God-being, spiritual-being, is the only being: "I am the Lord and beside me there is none else." "I am your God and besides me there is none other." Oneness is all there is.

Continue *feeling* (experiencing) your awareness. You may

understand it or feel it more as *presence.* Feel your *presence,* feel your energy, if you like; feel *you* "happening." Become aware of your Awareness Itself — the *substance* that is your awareness.

It does not matter what you are aware *of;* it has no consequence. There is no need to try to be rid of any particular thoughts or concerns; do not try to replace bad with good awareness. Go just a little deeper and feel Awareness Itself.

Now take this statement, this truth, gently into your mind: *Being aware of Awareness Itself is the key.*

The realization of this truth is not only the key but is the open door to the kingdom of infinity, the kingdom of unbounded and unconditional good — real, tangible and visible.

Being aware of Awareness Itself is the key and the open door to the kingdom of infinite good.

As you read these pages, as the message unfolds chapter by chapter, stay aware of Awareness Itself as best you can; keep your sense a little deeper than that which seems to be.

In other words, the voice of this message, your hearing of this message is actually your *being* this very message, this very truth, coming through as your fruition. This is what is actually happening. The message appears to come from teacher but there is no outer, separate teacher. Awareness Itself is teacher because Awareness Itself is all. The whole of God exists in and as your awareness. The presence you are, the awareness you have is the entirety of God being individual and unique you. Your entire universe exists within and as you. This message is the abundant bud, blossom, and fruit coming through into your awareness, filling the branches of your experience. You are hearing it; it is your truth, your awareness and your fruitage becoming the visible reality of your life.

Realize this truth. The way of it, the way of seeing it, and quickly so, is to keep going back (as best you can) just a bit more deeply within so that you are aware of Awareness It-self. There is no magic to it; simply pay attention to Aware-ness Itself rather than the things you are aware *of* in themselves.

In that state of being, you are open. You are standing right in the doorway of heaven, enabling (by standing in the doorway) heaven to see as and for you, to be your mind as and for you, to be your body as and for you, to be your world as and for you, to be your family, your partner, your husband, wife, relationship, your home, your business, your finances.

As we are there being aware of Awareness Itself, we are in that doorway enabling heaven or God or good, or truth, reality, existence itself, the creation itself (whatever word or synonym we wish to use) to be and see *for us*. As Saint Paul said, "I live, yet not I; Christ lives my life" — Buddha, spirit, truth lives my life, that which truly *is* lives me. This is the key.

When we start to feel the spark of awakening within and believe that it will take an immense spiritual realization or breakthrough for us to arrive at the place of freedom, it isn't true. We are awake now. We always have been, but we have been miseducated (unwittingly, of course) to believe that awakening takes a long time, maybe even many lifetimes. Spiritual teachings have unfortunately miseducated us.

Interestingly, the one teaching that never mentions a pe-riod of time involved in awakening is the Master's. I have always preferred to study the Master first and foremost. He is the one individual who has demonstrated the truth be-yond measure and revealed and taught every principle of doing so. In fact, he told us, "He that believeth on me, the works that I do shall he do also; and greater works than these shall he do." (John 14:12)

The only truth is oneness; the only truth is that I *am* that, not I can *become* that if I study enough, if I rise enough spir-itually, if I become a great spiritually realized being, and that

when I arrive at that point what the prophets say will become true for me; *then* I live yet not I, Christ or Buddha or
truth or God or good, reality, existence lives me; *then* I'll be
able to witness the multiplication of the loaves and fishes,
the healing of the body, unconditional love, wonderful harmony throughout my life, purpose fulfilled.

No! I *am* that, and that is *all* I am; that is *all* I ever have
been. In fact, *I am that* is all I possibly can be. I cannot be
anything else because the *I* that I am is the *one I* which is
God, good, reality, the one existence.

I can be, as a personal *sense* of self, *unaware* . . . yes.
There's the problem, but never am I not the whole kingdom
of good, the whole truth of existence.

That which I seek, that which I believe I do not have but
need, that which I am struggling with for a solution, a healing, sufficiency, prosperity, harmony, love, that which I
seek, *I already am.* "Son, [daughter,] you are ever with me,
and all that I have is yours," (Luke 15:31) not *will be* one day in
the future, not *can be* if you do A, B, or C. No, all that I have
is yours.

I am that I am. The place upon which you stand is holy
ground, even if it looks like disease, poverty, homelessness,
unhappiness, hopelessness; even if it looks like death, it is
not. There is no such reality as these, there is no death; there
is only harmony, wholeness and completeness; there is only
life and the fullness of life. "I am come that ye may have life,
and life more abundant."

I am come. . . . What does this mean? *I* am now permeating
your sense, your awareness, but hear it . . . *I am* come, not
you need to make me come, or find me somewhere. The
very *I* that we all are *is . . . is, is already* the whole kingdom of
good, perfectly real and visible, tangible, at every place
human sense deems good is needed, or healing is needed,
or sufficiency is needed, or love is needed, peace is needed.

Nothing is needed apart from our *awareness* of that which we already are and have. That is it, and the key to it is what we have heard: *Be aware of awareness itself,* not that which seems to be, not that which we believe we are aware of. Forget what we seem to be aware of. Good or bad, it isn't, in itself, that which is.

However, that which *is* — the one and only truth, the one and only truthful existence, the one and only truthful life, mind, body, place, amount — does not through our senses look different from our "human" and "world" form. It simply now looks truthful and acts harmoniously; it appears as it truly *is* — the image and likeness of God, good.

We all still recognize each other; we all still recognize our homes, our businesses, our neighbors, our universe. Except . . . as *Awareness Itself* sees for us and as us, experiences for us and as us, *is* for us and as us, we see the universe as it truly is; we see each other as we truly are — divine spiritual being, spiritual mind, spiritual body that cannot be diseased or injured. We and our bodies are immune — untouchable by the world and yet perfectly visible to both material sense that does not and cannot see its truth and to us as spiritual or Awareness-Itself beings simply aware of the truth of being and the world we live in. "I am in the world but not of it," the Master says, and we can say it too. We know it too; we experience it as soon as we are living by *Awareness Itself* instead of a personal sense of self.

God Consciousness; Realizing God

Long ago I spent years trying to grasp and live by this term "God consciousness," and failing miserably. What is God consciousness? What is "realized God"? I had so much trouble with that word "realize" or "realized." How do I *realize* God? I had no idea. This, by the way, just like you, is after reading hundreds of books and listening to scores of classes, just as most truth students have done. After all my effort I still had no idea how to realize God or how to live as God consciousness. The fruits of God consciousness were nowhere to be seen in my life.

I obviously did not realize God; I did not have God consciousness. Then one day, I saw that there is an enormous difference between our *sense* of consciousness (that which we have been educated to believe is our consciousness) and that which consciousness *actually is.*

It was clear that if God is one, if truly, truly God is *one* and there is nothing other than that oneness, then, of course, everything is that one. There cannot be anything else; there cannot be anything different whatsoever, anywhere throughout the infinitude, if it is true that God is the one and the only.

So starting with that principle, accepting it as literal fact, I understood that there cannot be two different states of consciousness. There cannot be God consciousness and then human consciousness. There cannot be capital-C Consciousness and lower-c consciousness in oneness. Where would two different states exist in oneness? Unless, of course, oneness was really twoness, in which case it never was oneness to begin with. Be assured, there is but one consciousness, and it is God.

Then I realized something which was a mighty awakening for me. *I can certainly, in personal sense, be less or poorly aware of consciousness . . .* yes. I could entertain a poor *awareness* of consciousness. I could have a dark or dim or foggy awareness or *sense* of the consciousness *I am,* which is God.

That, I saw, is my problem — not that God is not the fullness of its consciousness, meaning that God is everywhere present right here and now; that God is the only *I* that *I am* because God is the one and the only existence.

This must be true and is true. God is the only mind; God is the only body.

There is not more than one body. If God is one, God is the only, God is the infinitude, God is the omnipresence, God is the eternity, then there cannot be anything else or different or separate or less; and indeed, there is not. This body is the one body *individually sensed . . . yes,* nevertheless the one body.

All of us could step into one ocean yet we would each have individual experience. It is undeniable. Not one of us would fail to have our own individual experience of the one ocean. The water I would be in is not my water, separate or different from your water. It is the same ocean, yet individually experienced. And this is true of what we actually are — the one God, the one infinitude, the one consciousness *individually experiencing.*

I realized that the whole secret, therefore, of evidencing good — of healing, prosperity, love, peace, and harmony throughout the universe (my universe, my individual sense of the one universe, the one infinity) — is to *awaken to* that which *is;* not to believe that I do not *have* that which is, but to *awaken to* that which *is.*

This is what the Master is instructing us when he says, "Whosoever hath not, from him shall be taken away even that which he hath." To those who are unaware that the *I* of them is God, who are unaware that the *I* of them constitutes all that God is and has, who are unaware that the whole kingdom of God is within them as the very *I* of them, even that which they have depletes, becomes old, decrepit, unreliable, turns into lack and limitation.

We all know it is true, that at some stage in the experience of the personal self we age and eventually die, and usually along the way, we suffer: we may find our body diseased; we may become weak and lose some of our faculties; we may experience pain and suffering — as a personal self.

However, the Master gives us the secret. "Whosoever *hath,* to him shall be given, and he shall have more abundance." An abundance of truth shall be ours. What does this mean? We *awaken* ever more to that which *is.* Our spiritual eyes are opened ever wider and we *see* as reality and practicality ever more of our truthful being, our truthful mind, body and world, our truthful husband, wife, partner, love, family, home, business, finances.

We *have* an infinity of good in every category of life because the kingdom of God is within us. When we are *aware* of this truth we *see* ever more of our infinity. We also experience ever more of our eternal life.

Death does not exist. Life is the only existence. God is life, and God is the only — invariable, eternal. God is the eternal now. If you are alive now, you are alive for eternity because now is eternity. Eternity does not stretch off into the future somewhere or somehow. Eternity is now. Eternity is the very *I* of the I that is you. And what is the *I?* It is *Awareness Itself.*

As you lift away from personal sense, as you detach from the belief of person, thing, condition, place, amount, and activity being real in themselves, into *Awareness Itself,* and as you start feeling, start experiencing, Awareness Itself living itself as you and for you, that is when you start experiencing your truth, the fulfillment and eternity you are, in real and practical terms.

We start discovering our fulfilling purpose on earth. We start witnessing the miracles of life, at least so-called miracles to material sense. The impossible seems to start happening. Very often the "miracles" of life seem normal and natural unfoldments or "coincidences," and they *are,* in truth. Wonderful, timely good shows up just where and when it's needed, through the normal channels or activities of our world. Nothing about our world and its ways is different from God, from truth, from fulfillment at every step; but to material sense it seems so. To material sense, God experience is a miracle. To those who live in truth, all is the boundlessness of that which *is.*

Truthful life is wondrous, joyous, boundless and unconditional, but not a miracle. God is the truth of existence, which is not a miracle but simply that which *is* (just as math simply *is;* the harmony of 4 x 4 = 16 is not a miracle, but simply the *is* of math. The same is true of the truth, the principle that is God).

I once heard a spiritual teacher talk about "divine intervention." There is no such thing. Divinity cannot intervene any more than math can. There is nothing to intervene in or for or to, because all *is* divine, all *is* God, all *is* truth, already.

Realize, realize . . . all *is* the kingdom of truth. You *are,* the very *I* you *are,* the very awareness you are aware *with,* is the kingdom of God, good — fully finished, fully perfect, fully evident, fully visible right where you are. The whole of infinity and omnipresence exists fully manifested, fully demonstrated, fully visible as you and right where you are. The *I* of you is that; the awareness you are aware *with* is that — is the consciousness of God or God consciousness — is God, is consciousness, the one consciousness which is God.

Let us rest with this for a few minutes, and feel awareness happening.

(A few moments of stillness and receptivity)

Be aware a little more deeply than thought or what your thought is attached to, where your concerns are, or your sense of desire or need is. All your concerns will be met in the pages of this book, my friend, and, in fact, already are as you hold the book and soak in the consciousness that comes with it.

Again, be aware more deeply than your thoughts or your personal sense of awareness, and be aware of *Awareness Itself.*

Truly relax. Let go in it. You have nothing to be concerned about. Awareness Itself is your life, is your protector, is your safety, is your security, is your guard, is your castle. Nothing of the world can get in, nothing can damage you, can hurt you, can destroy you. So relax, let go, and simply feel Awareness Itself happening.

After a few minutes of rest and relaxation, feeling the presence of Awareness Itself, do your best not to involve yourself in human conversation, not to go out into the world, but to honor your awakening to Awareness Itself.

Protect yourself, keep yourself in swaddling clothes, stay aware of Awareness Itself as consistently as you can. Do not watch or read the news. Avoid it for as long as you can, or completely. You will have far greater and quicker awakening if you keep yourself out of "this world" as much as possible.

CHAPTER TWO

THE SPACE IN BETWEEN

A wonderful way of practicing and becoming masterful at living Awareness Itself is this: Look into your room. Focus on something a little distance away from you, maybe the opposite wall or a picture on the wall, or an object in your room.

At the level of sense alone, *we* are located *here* observing an object *over there* with a faculty we have called *awareness.* Actually, Awareness Itself is all "three" — the existence called *you,* the object you are aware *of,* and the faculty of awareness *itself.* Awareness Itself is all. As you observe the object, realize that Awareness is alive as all that constitutes your universe, making this experience possible.

Awareness Is All

Without awareness you would be dead; your entire life would be non-existent. Everything of your existence is awareness. Not one person, thing or condition in your universe is taking place without awareness. In other words, if you are unaware of a person, thing or condition can you prove it exists?

Your whole existence is *awareness.*

Realize this truth as you observe the object.

Now look around your room and realize that all you experience is itself the substance, faculty, and form of awareness.

Become aware of your awareness "happening."

Now look again throughout your room and become aware of the hundreds of details of which it is made — different objects, shapes, forms, colors, fragrances, sizes, weights, positions, sounds (inside and outside; human sounds, animal sounds, nature sounds, weather sounds). If you are with another person you are aware of his or her breathing, body, size, color, character, beauty. We could carry on exploring the many details that constitute the room in which you sit, but our interest is the substance and faculty of *awareness* of which experience is made.

Our universal awareness is possible only because of Awareness Itself. Realize that all of experience is possible only, is happening only, because of the substance and faculty of *awareness.*

The Space in Between

Look at the far end of your room — at the wall, a painting, a bookshelf, a floor lamp. Now become aware of the *space between* what you sense as *you* and *it.* Pull your awareness back halfway between you and it. Begin to *feel,* to become more aware of that middle point where seemingly there is nothing but thin air, but where actually there is the fullness of Awareness Itself. You are now becoming aware of the substance of Awareness Itself.

Awareness has no shape, no size, no weight, no color, no sound, no smell, no character, no amount, no quality, no location. Awareness simply *is*.

As you become aware of Awareness Itself, you quickly begin to feel a freedom; you feel a peace and spaciousness because you have unencumbered your awareness. It has no *thing* in it. Keep looking at it, in the middle of what seems to be you and the object you were focusing on. You have pulled back into the middle where there seems to be nothing but unencumbered space. You are free, and you quickly feel that freedom.

You have released your sense from having to process *things*. Now return your gaze to the far wall or the object, and instantly you have re-engaged a process. Your senses are busy again; your memory is busy reporting what is familiar to you about that wall or that thing.

We can do the same with anything we see, hear, taste, touch or smell. Your senses busily report what it is you're observing, what it's for, what it's doing there, what size, color, and shape it is. Of course, at the level of appearance the reports are quite accurate and useful, but at the level of Awareness Itself they are entirely wrong. You are not what you seem to be, in yourself; the wall is not what it seems to be, in itself; the object is not what it seems to be, in itself. All is Awareness Itself.

No person, thing, amount, business, place, home is what it appears to be in and of its own self. Sense testimony without a knowledge of truth is valuable only at the material level of awareness but has nothing to do with truth.

This is why the Master said, "Judge not according to the appearance, but judge righteous judgment". In other words, know that all is God despite appearance. That word *despite* has been a major word from the first Miracle Self teaching. It is a wonderful word. *Despite* the way he, she, or it appears to be, and what appears to be needed, all is God.

God is the only existence, which means that infinity, om-nipresence, eternity, harmony, peace, wonder, joy, whole-ness and freedom are present where, to sense testimony alone, good or bad material form appears to be.

As soon as we disengage the processing of sense testi-mony or the intellect, we feel the freedom of non-processed awareness.

Now again pull back right into the middle of your room and feel the freedom of awareness that has nothing in it to process.

Be aware of the space in the middle of the room and re-alize that nothing is good about it and nothing is bad about it. It just *is.* It is innocent and impotent.

It is almost (not quite, but almost) free of every name in the language, of every definition that exists.

Freedom and Peace

The reason we feel a freedom, a peace, is that the moment we unencumber our existence, our awareness, we are tapping into Awareness Itself. We are now unencumbered awareness, unencumbered consciousness, unencumbered existence.

In other words, awareness (consciousness, existence) without name, without definition, without good or bad be-lieved about it, simply *is.* As soon as we have attained a state of awareness that we can call *is,* we are there; we're standing in the doorway of heaven, and the door is wide open.

When we exist with belief, with name and definition, with judgment or opinion of either good or bad, we are fully encumbered. There is no way we can experience God or Good in that encumbered state of awareness.

This became an early practice of mine. I would spend every possible moment with my awareness withdrawn from the people, things, and conditions of my world. Each time, and for as long as I kept it up, I experienced freedom. Soon, with regular hourly practice, we become masterful at remaining detached from the things of awareness, in Awareness Itself.

We will always sense the people and things of the world. The secret is to realize that sense testimony alone is false evidence. Even sense testimony devoid of belief is nothing but a *concept* of God, not God Itself. As we withdraw from all people and things of awareness, into Awareness Itself, we are seeking the kingdom of God aright, and now we never need to take thought for or have concern for appearance. In Awareness Itself all true appearance is taken care of automatically and infallibly.

To withdraw from that which seems to be, it helps to close your eyes to it. Then, purely as an act of awareness, pull into the space in between and rest there.

This is easy when we are sitting at home or at our desks or in the garden. But what about when we're in the world? What about when we're working, when we're with our love, our family, when we're at home, when we're shopping, driving, in conversation? What do we do?

If you are with another person now look at him or her. If you are not, select an object to look at; or if you hear noises, then be aware of them. Now close your eyes and withdraw from the attachment to the he or she or it of appearance. Gently pull back in awareness and become more attentive to, more fully aware of the space in between.

Now reopen your eyes and keep your awareness in the middle space. Rest there for a few minutes. Feel the freedom and spaciousness of non-attachment.

You can do this as you're walking, as you're working, as you're on the telephone, even as you are talking with someone. People cannot detect what you're doing. We can be looking at each other, talking with each other, and completely unable to detect that our awareness is pulled back a little and we're more aware of the space between us than of each other. No one can tell that.

Now we are free of having to process, being tempted to judge, having an opinion, or listening to memory. I do not want to remember anything about you because it would be a lie; it would be a falsity. I want the new experience, the fresh manna. God is ever new, ever fresh. Therefore, our awareness is ever new, ever fresh, and when we are consciously aware of this truth and keep our awareness free and open to it, we evidence it. I want to have an ever-renewed experience of Awareness Itself revealing who you really are to me. I do not want to rely on belief, concept or memory to experience who you are because it will be false experience.

I do not want to remember what money is, what my business is, what my teaching is, my students are, my friends are (I do not have any human friends left, thank goodness. I have you though, my true friends, my spiritual family, and I treasure you, each and every one). I do not want to remember what my home is, the things in my home are, my neighbors and neighborhood are, because if I run by memory, concept or belief, I am living a false experience, and in that false experience I can't find God. God is not available in the false experience, the believed experience, the conceptual experience in itself. God is available as tangible and practical experience only as we are being what It is, which is Awareness Itself.

More Practice

Turn your awareness back to the space in between, and be free. *Feel* the freedom of being unencumbered by people, things, and conditions.

(Rest in the silence of Awareness Itself for a few minutes)

I see you but not with my physical sense. I do not want to rely on physical sense to experience you. The real you is Awareness Itself so I want to exist in and as Awareness Itself, letting it reveal itself as you to me.

Then I see and have your truth; and if for any reason you are struggling with a problem, the presence of Awareness Itself taking place in "me" lifts and illumines "you," and you are freed.

Try to describe the space in between, the space of pure awareness. You will struggle.

Awareness Itself or God or truth or reality, spirit, is utterly indescribable. We can never contain God, truth, and describe it. We can only name and describe something contained. We believe we understand who he or she or it is because we have accepted appearance at face value. Appearance suggests that every person or thing is an entity in itself, a contained life or form, a personal or definite describable existence. Because we have believed appearance as being real, we have named and defined it all. We have attached labels to every person and thing and we judge by those labels. But God, being the infinitude, omnipresence, spirit and truth — the incorporeal — is utterly indescribable, uncontainable, un-nameable.

As we become more aware of the space in between, we also become less able to name and define our world, and in this state of awareness we are very much more in conscious oneness with God.

You see how, in just these few minutes, we have pulled away from that which seems to be, to become more aware of the space in between. Realize that the space in between is almost impossible to name or define. Therefore, we are much more deeply conscious of our oneness with God in that one move. Every time we struggle to name and define our experience, we are more at-one with God, more open and receptive to being able to see our good, to evidence our healing, our prosperity, our peace, our harmony, because Awareness Itself and the visible form of it are one and the very same experience.

There is no such thing as unformed God or Awareness, invisible God or Awareness, intangible God or Awareness. "I and the father are one." "If you see me, you see the Father who sent me [who is the true form of me you witness]."

Make sure you realize this. There is no such thing as unformed God or Awareness. If there were, God would be two different states of existence or entities, and that is untrue. There is only *one* — *one* God, *one* infinitude, *one* omnipresence, *one* existence, *one* state of being. "I am the Lord, and beside me there is none else." Nothing is hidden, separate or different in the mind of God — in Awareness Itself.

It is logical that Awareness Itself is fully aware of itself. How could Awareness Itself be unaware? How could consciousness be unconscious, or partly conscious and partly unconscious? Such a belief is nonsensical.

Awareness Itself or consciousness is the infinitude, is the omnipresence, is the one existence, is the one reality. As Thomas Troward said in the *Edinburgh Lectures,* "The whole of the infinite is present at each point of itself at the same time". Indeed, nothing is absent or hidden in the mind of God, in the consciousness of infinity. Nothing is hidden in Awareness Itself because Awareness Itself *is* every point of the infinite at the same time.

Awareness Itself Is Aware As and For Us

This is the key to awakening. As we lift more and more each day into and experience the presence of Awareness Itself filling us, and as we yield our sense of awareness to Awareness Itself, everything of good becomes visible and tangible to our sense.

Nothing of good, nothing of truth, can remain hidden from our sense for very long as we live as and by Awareness Itself because Awareness Itself *is* the all-good and is being aware as and for us.

In other words, healing, prosperity, love, peace, and harmony infallibly come through, whether quickly or slowly, as we live by Awareness Itself because Awareness Itself is the all-of-all good now enabled to see Itself "through" our emptied and yielded window of being.

Yielding our sense of being to Awareness Itself is the key to what has been called demonstration. No experience of diseased or discordant person, thing or condition can remain so very long in the presence of Awareness Itself. Awareness Itself (God) is the omnipresent all-good. "God saw everything that he had made, and behold, it was very good." (Genesis 1:31) All good already *is*. Nothing *becomes* good; nothing changes from bad to good; nothing actually heals, prospers, harmonizes, pacifies, even though it appears to according to objective sense. All the good of infinity is omnipresent where you are this instant. The only thing that clouds it from your senses is the unwittingly accepted belief in separation and difference from Awareness Itself.

Realize that "your" awareness is, in fact, Awareness Itself, as the sunbeam is, in fact, the sun. Yield your sense of awareness to that which it truly is. Awareness Itself is omniactive as itself as individual and unique you, so there is no need to fear or to be doubtful about letting go and yielding your entire self to it. Let Awareness Itself be and see itself, in its own way as you and for you. Then, as you feel the presence flowing or glowing within, the objective sense of it is quickly witnessed as the "outer" good right where it needs to be as your fulfillment of experience.

––––––––––––––

Look into your room again. Keep your eyes open, and become aware of the in-between space.

Now become aware of your peripheral awareness which is full of objects, names, definitions, beliefs, concepts, memories, ideas, needs, desires. All of these exist only as objective sense. Everything we believe is real and worthy and have attached to, and everything we believe we sense as being needed or desired is objective. It has a name, a definition; it is a person, thing, condition, or amount; it is finite, local; it occupies an amount of space somewhere and exists at a certain date and time. In other words, none of it has anything to do with God — with what all actually *is*.

"Instant" Freedom in Awareness Itself

As spiritual students, we have struggled to be free of all that is untrue — free of all the things and conditions we have just identified, and more. We have devoted years or decades to the search for truth and the way of practical truth experience. We have mostly failed *because we have been searching for that which we already are and have.*

As we awaken out of the hypnotism of belief, we experience instantaneous freedom and harmony of all. Why? Belief and its false forms of life are not of God, therefore have no law or principle to sustain themselves in our lives. Everything we can name and define is a belief-thing. Even though it appears to be real as we believe it to be, it isn't. It is substance-less, formless, lawless, principle-less. It is nothing in and of its own self.

This is why it dissipates into the nothingness it is when the presence of Awareness Itself is brought to the scene. As dark dissipates in the presence of light and leaves no "scars" or "smell of smoke," so every bad and good we have believed is real in itself dissipates in the presence of Awareness Itself.

Freedom is instant because belief — good and bad — is not an entity, therefore offers no resistance to truth. Belief is like thin air — acquiescent — when it is known for the nothingness it actually is, and when the presence of Awareness Itself is brought to it.

You can experience freedom this instant. Pull your awareness away from all objects into the middle space and stay there. Become aware of the middle space to the point where you feel the presence of it, where you feel you are at one with it. Allow your senses to become filled with the presence and feel of this space, empty of *things*.

Rest there for a few minutes, abiding in it and letting it abide in you until you feel free.

There it is. You are instantly free as you *feel* the freedom, the quiet, the spaciousness. You are free because you no longer have human beings and material things and conditions in your awareness. You are free because there is nothing for you to need or desire in Awareness Itself. You are free because you are no longer holding onto things, and no longer needing or desiring this or that from those things.

You are in a no-things awareness, a non-attached awareness, enjoying awareness just for the sake of the experience. And because Awareness Itself is the all-of-all good, your no-thing, non-attached state of awareness is itself the open presence of you which enables the infinite good to be seen.

The very minute you find yourself pulled back from objects, more fully aware of the space in between, you have freed yourself from the entire world.

It has to be *felt*. You cannot achieve it *physically*. It is not enough to simply withdraw your physical focus from things and believe you are detached from the world and open spiritually. Everything of spiritual realization is about *feeling*. Withdraw your sense attachment from objects and gently, patiently *feel* the presence of the middle space, that empty space, that seemingly thin air in between you and objects, the people and things of the world.

You are free of all in this world the moment you feel the presence of Awareness Itself. Do you see that? Awareness is all; therefore what fills your awareness *is* your tangibly experienced all. The moment you *feel* free, rested and relaxed in Awareness Itself, you are free. That is the moment you are free of disease because disease, which is physical, requires a physical body to attach itself to and live — a defined body, an objective entity. Like breeds like. When we are aware physically (when we believe that the physical body is real in itself) we are exposed and vulnerable to the entire physical world of good and bad. We can be physically healthy or physically sick. We cannot avoid it. Like breeds like. We will always exist with one or another of these experiences.

But the moment we awaken to the truth that Awareness Itself is all of all, and that the physical body is nothing more than an objective *sense* of that which is one hundred percent Awareness Itself; and then begin to live detached from the objective and free in Awareness Itself, we are free of the entire world of good vs. bad.

Whatsoever we attach to on earth, we lock truth out of in our experience, whereas whatsoever we release on earth in the awareness of Awareness Itself, we open for the evidence of harmony. "Verily I say unto you, Whatsoever ye shall bind on earth shall be bound in heaven: and whatsoever ye shall loose on earth shall be loosed in heaven." (Matthew 18:18)

There is no way for heaven, truth, reality, to be evident while we are attached to names, things, conditions, opinions, beliefs any more than it is possible to take off and fly while being bolted to the ground. There is no way for God to be evident finitely, for a personal self, a personal problem, in a local place, because God is the infinitude, and infinity cannot fit into finiteness.

The infinitude is omnipresent, the whole of itself present and visible at every point of itself at the same time. Infinity cannot be divided and separated into little, personal aspects of infinity named you and me. We cannot take a slice of infinity and use it to heal our bodies, prosper our businesses, feed our families or friends or the multitudes. It is impossible. Infinity is one, indivisible and inseparable. We either seek infinity as it is for what it is, or we seek finiteness and find ourselves with none. God is indivisible. God is one, whole, and complete, and that is the only way truth is evidence-able — as itself, infinity as infinity.

Infinity, truth, is evidence-able only as the whole of itself. It cannot be used finitely as the healing of my body, the sufficiency of my finances, the love of my relationship, the health or healing of my friend or my students, the safety of my home. That is like believing that the sun can give me personal sunbeams to light and heat my Sunday afternoon despite my neighbors being rained out. It is not only impossible but ludicrous to imagine.

Our desire for fulfillment is perfectly true. There is nothing wrong with wanting good health, sufficient money or even an abundance of wealth, successful business, happy loving relationship, a peaceful, secure home, and safe world. It is perfectly natural to want the good things of life — that yearning to have our fulfillment, freedom, love, harmony, peace — because they make for a fuller, more creative life.

Our natural inclination is toward fulfillment. Every breath we breathe is actually the impulse toward the experience of truth. This inherent impulse, in a nutshell, explains every human behavior, good or bad. It is Psychology 101, but the psychologists do not realize it. Everything the so-called human being does, good or bad (or even unwitting), is the natural impulse toward the experience of truth. It comes out in an infinite variety of ways, colored by the degree of the individual's awareness — some good, some bad, some glorious, some atrocious. In truth, we must harbor no judgment or condemnation. We understand that human behavior is governed by collective belief just as we understand that the behavior of a hypnotized person is governed by the hypnotist.

Seeking fulfillment is either unwittingly (for human beings) or wittingly (for truth students) the activity of God in us. If we are unable to interpret it, the drive for fulfillment can result in either good or bad behavior. As soon as we understand truth we start seeking aright — God for the experience of God fulfillment rather than God for a human or material fulfillment.

Evidencing the Infinity of Being

There is only one way to evidence who we truly are and what our infinite resources and capabilities are. We must discover and awaken to our true identity. If we attempt to bring God or infinity into our finite belief about who we are and what our world is, we fail.

In the same way, if we wish to fly, we must discover the universal laws of aerodynamics and abide by them. It is of no use attempting to make our automobile fly, and it is of as little use attempting to discover aerodynamics in our country but not in every country of the world. We cannot achieve it. We cannot get aerodynamics to work for a non-aerodynamic vehicle, or personally for our own good but not the universal good.

We have to understand that aerodynamics is one, universal, and omnipresent. Aerodynamics is principle. Wherever we are in the world, there the fullness of aerodynamics is. We have to understand that we cannot slice aerodynamics into little pieces and use one of those pieces personally to fly from here to there. Such a feat is impossible. Either aerodynamics is tapped into as its wholeness, thereby enabling us to fly all over the world whenever we want to, or we have none, and we cannot fly anywhere. There is no middle ground, no choice. We either have the whole or we have none.

The same applies to truth. We either have the whole of truth or we have none. So we have to discover what that whole is, how it works, how to experience it. The minute we do, we have all that infinity is and has at hand.

As with any principle, the moment we understand our true identity (God or infinity) and abide by it, we have the full benefit of it at any and every instant. We are able to instantly open to life, open to love, open to abundance, open to harmony, open to peace because we now understand what existence is. We are not attempting to get existence, get truth or God, to do us favors, to work for us personally, despite every other person in our awareness. We have awakened to the fact that God is one, the infinitude, the omnipresence, the eternity; and so the only way we can experience truth is *as it is.* We experience infinity *as infinity is,* never as finiteness or for a finite condition — in other words, never for something we can name or define.

We are never required to hold a name or definition in mind in order to witness truth. All is God already. All we have to do is lift our awareness into that which all *is.* Remember, judge not by the appearance because the appearance has nothing to do (or let's say very little to do) with that which all actually *is.* If we believe appearance at face value and then attempt to demonstrate God to bring health and harmony to that appearance, we fail.

However, as we awaken to the truth that, despite sense testimony, all is God, all is good, all is reality, all is spirit, and then open to that allness (God, Awareness Itself, infinity, omnipresence, spirit) letting it be aware for us — letting it reveal to our sense what *it is* as appearing person, thing, and condition — we witness it.

Let us yield our sense, our faculties of seeing, hearing, tasting, touching, smelling, our thought, our belief, our opinions. Let us yield the whole of us. Let us release the personal sense of self, and give our entire being to that which *is.* The very act of releasing earth is the act of heaven made evident. And the way of it, the way of avoiding the difficulty with the word *God* or the phrase *God consciousness* or *God realization,* is to understand God as *Awareness Itself.* I don't know about you, but I had difficulty with the terms *God* or *God Consciousness,* and as I look among the students and hear from you, we all have the same difficulties. What is God? What is God consciousness? The words and the phrases are so loaded with orthodoxy, misunderstanding and miseducation that they are difficult to get past. So we'll find another way. The word doesn't matter. God or Awareness — what does it matter? So let us use the word Awareness or the phrase Awareness Itself.

Whatsoever Ye Bind on Earth

Let us hear the Master again: Whatsoever ye bind on earth (whatsoever we believe is real in itself, and attach our hopes, desires, and reliances to) is locked in heaven. Heaven is unavailable to our sense, even though we exist on earth as it is in heaven twenty-four hours a day. Nevertheless, the visible, practical experience is locked from our sense by *our* believing and attaching to the things of sense testimony. Since as far back as we can recall we have been taught to believe appearance, and so we have developed a sense of need and desire *for the things of appearance in themselves.*

This is our trouble. We believe the people, things, activities, and conditions of sense; we believe we know what is real; we believe we know what is intelligent and what is unintelligent, what is reasonable and what is unreasonable, what is possible and what is impossible in our believed reality. Many sincere people and organizations even believe they know what God is and what God is not. Every minute of belief entertained in awareness binds us to that belief which binds truth from our experience.

However, whatsoever ye *release* on earth is *released* in heaven — not will one day be released but *is instantaneously* released. Heaven is fully evident the instant we truly release earth.

There is a direct and immediate way of releasing earth. Pull your awareness back from that which seems to be, pull back from the people, objects and subjects of appearance, the amounts and the activities, the names and definitions themselves, and get into that middle space of awareness — seemingly between you and them, between you and the world. Bring your awareness into the thin air in the middle and *feel* its presence.

The whole of God is right there; the whole kingdom of

good is right there. The seemingly empty space of awareness is fully God-aware and visible. Awareness Itself *is* God.

As we have unencumbered ourselves (as we have released earth and are abiding in the empty space, this middle
space which we find almost impossible to describe, feeling
Awareness Itself), we are at-one with God. We feel it
quickly; we feel the peace of it; we feel the freedom of it; we
feel unencumbered; we feel as if all the burdens we have
been carrying around have fallen from our shoulders. It is
an almost instant release.

Now, if we stay there for five seconds, we are free for
only five seconds; if we stay there for five minutes, we are
free for five minutes; if we stay there for an hour, we are free
for an hour. When we have reached the stage of being able
to maintain the released state, feeling the presence of
Awareness Itself all day and all night, we are free forever.

Can any of us, I myself included, remain in Awareness Itself one hundred percent? No, probably not yet. But we can
achieve ninety, ninety-five, ninety-eight percent of every
hour if we are truly devoted to living and serving the God
life. It is surprising, after a little regular practice, how natural it is to stay almost completely released from appearance
even while we are active in our work, with our family, doing
our shopping, engaged in conversation. We quickly become
quite masterful at continually re-pulling back to the middle
space and there maintain our freedom of being and world.

The more we practice the more we develop a taste for it
that will not easily let us abandon the practice. We quickly
feel a constant impulse to get back into the peace and freedom of Awareness Itself; and the more we abide in it, the
more it is felt abiding in us. It is this experience — of Awareness Itself felt abiding in us — that releases and evidences
the infinity of being.

We are unable to experience the infinity of being while

we are closed spiritually, interested and engaged humanly, materially, physically, while just about everything that fills our sense is nameable and definable, finite and personal; while our minds are filled with what we need, what we desire, what we have to achieve, what we wish to be free of. This state of being is spiritually closed. The windows of our soul are shut tight and the light of heaven cannot enter to reveal what life truly is, who we truly are, what our business truly is, what our home and our family truly are, what our purpose truly is, what our earth truly is. We are attached to that which seems to be; we are bound to earth.

So the more we fill each hour with pulling away from that which seems to be, existing in or as (or being more aware of) the space in between, and relaxing, feeling it — this is the key — we are in God and God is in us, which means God is in our experience. In truth, we are always in God and God is always in us. God is the only presence, the only life, the only form; however, remember, it is our *conscious awareness of the presence of God* instead of the presence of that which seems to be, that makes God real and visible as our tangible experience.

God Can Only Do For Us
What It Can Do Through Us

God can only do for us what it can do through us. The fact that God is the only existence, the only reality, the only presence does not help us. The fact that truth *is,* is not enough to make it tangibly evident.

The great secret is to "know the truth, and the truth will make you free." That truth is that God is Awareness Itself. Therefore, it is by an *act of awareness* that we tune "ourselves" with what Self truly is. When our awareness is tuned and yielded to Awareness Itself, the infinity of Awareness Itself pours through "us" and we quickly discover the life abundant.

"Abide in me, and I in you. As the branch cannot bear fruit of itself, except it abide in the vine; no more can ye, except ye abide in me. I am the vine, ye are the branches: He that abideth in me, and I in him, the same bringeth forth much fruit: for without me ye can do nothing." (John 15:4-5)

As we yield our sense of awareness, Awareness Itself sees itself for us, presents itself to us as all persons, things, conditions, and activities in our experience. This is the only way God or good becomes evident: when it sees itself for us, when "I live, yet not I; Christ lives my life," Buddha lives my life, Awareness Itself lives my life; when the one reality, the one existence, the one life lives itself as itself as us, through us, and for us.

Only truth sees itself; only spirit sees itself; only God sees itself; only Awareness Itself sees the true image and likeness. If we attempt to evidence truth, we fail. If we believe we know what life is, what he, she and it are, and attempt to evidence their truth, we fail.

We cannot see truth no matter how much we meditate and sit in silence; however, when we lift into Awareness Itself and then let It get on with the job, the miracle of truth is quickly evident, real and practical.

Live *being aware of* the space in between. Feel the freedom; feel the unencumbered self. Release yourself from the world in this way and know that *in* this way, heaven is released as individual you.

CHAPTER THREE

AWARENESS IS ALL

Awareness is *all*. We have heard it termed as God is all, consciousness is all, the infinitude, omnipresence, spirit, is all. Now let us realize it as *Awareness is all*.

God is consciousness. A synonym is awareness. The infinitude is Awareness Itself and has only itself about it, in it, happening as it. The whole of the infinitude is awareness, has nothing but awareness in it, and exists fully at every point of itself at the same time. Every point of the infinitude is fully aware of the entirety of itself *as itself* at the same time.

Just imagine. Look at the tip of your finger, and realize that the whole of infinity exists right there and is fully aware of the whole of itself as what appears to sense as your fingertip.

Look at an object in your room, and realize the whole of infinity is there and is fully aware of itself as itself as what appears to sense to be the object or that point of observation.

Now pull back to the middle space between you and the object and realize that the space is the whole of the infinitude being fully aware of itself as itself — meaning that the whole of God is right there fully present, fully aware of the whole of itself as that seemingly small volume of awareness, the middle place, the place in between. The whole kingdom of God, the whole kingdom of heaven and earth and all the host of them, exist right there. Nothing more of God exists outside of or beyond right here.

As you and I are aware of Awareness Itself right there (this middle space or the space in between), we *have* God awareness. We are in God consciousness.

It is impossible to have a *little* God consciousness versus a *fullness* because God is one, infinite, omnipresent, indivisible, and inseparable. Even when it seems that we have just a little awareness of Awareness Itself, it isn't true. Judge not by your sense, your belief, but by Awareness Itself.

If you are aware of Awareness Itself by bringing your awareness to the middle space, unencumbering your senses of things and feeling the presence, you *have* God consciousness. You have yielded your sense to Awareness Itself and you feel it. God is glowing in you.

There is no objectivity in God. Objectivity is simply our material sense of that which is one hundred percent immaterial. We are having a corporeal sense of that which is one hundred percent incorporeal. Corporeal sense (or objective, material sense) is nothing of its own self, is not an entity, has not changed God or Awareness into a different entity, presence or experience.

God is God, and God is nothing more or less than God, and God can only *be* God because there is nothing else in all of existence to be. Because God is only God, and there is nothing else but God, there is nothing that can change God. If there were something that could change God, it would mean that that something is greater than God, which is, of course, nonsense. It would take a power greater than

God to change God, would it not?

Only God is; only Awareness Itself is. Not only is God the only existence, but God is the only power. Even in believed sensory experience, which seems to have many powers, God is omnipotence, the almighty one power.

Let us realize that God is the one, the almighty, the omnipotence, the omniscience, the omnipresence, the infinitude, the only. As we *sense* God as objective experience (which is our current degree of awareness, one of many mansions in my Father's house, one of the infinite degrees of awareness) it does not mean that that which is incorporeal has been changed into corporeal people and things. We simply have a corporeal sense. That is all. God has not been changed.

Even that which appears objective to our sense is actually infinite, non-objective. That which seems to be local, finite, is not local and finite. It cannot be because there is *only* infinity and omnipresence.

As we look at each other, we are observing the infinity, omnipresence, and eternity of being, not a human being, not a local being, not a temporal being, not a physical being with a mental mind, but the infinity of being, the eternity of being. There isn't another type of being. Only infinity, omnipresence and eternity exist; therefore being is *that*. If there were another type of being, God would have to be two, not one — one being infinity and the other being finite, one being omnipresent and the other being locally present, one being eternal and the other being temporal.

No, God is *one,* the only, which means that you are that one and only, I am that one and the only, every person and thing in our entire consciousness is that one and that only. Therefore, despite our *sense* of things, all is infinite, omnipresent, eternal.

Sense testimony in and of its own self is untrue. That which seems to be real in and of its own self is not real. Only

God is; therefore only God is reality. Only infinity is (and all the other synonyms), and that which God is is Awareness Itself or *aliveness* or *consciousness*.

The *awareness* that I am is God, is the truth of me. The very awareness that I am aware *with* is God, is the truth of me and of everything I am aware *of.*

Now let's realize something about awareness. This realization is your quick and powerful freedom. It is your good made evident this hour; it is the opening of the spiritual eyes enabling you to clearly see that which *is.*

First, realize that Awareness is all, that nothing exists except Awareness Itself. As we observe the objective sense of each other, we are actually observing the one being and body of Awareness, in its infinite variety of sensed form. What seems to be a mind and a body, isn't; it is awareness alone. We have unfortunately labeled the infinite variety of people and things that constitute our universe. If we had not done so, if we had stuck with only God — God is all, Awareness is all — we would probably not be living the hypnotized state we have lived since the "beginning of time."

As soon as we place another word alongside God or Awareness Itself, we are in trouble because we have created a sense of separation. We now have God *and.* We've made a concept of that which *is,* and we start believing that concept; we start examining it, desiring things from it, believing it can be good or bad.

We have done this with the mind and body. We have believed the mind is separate and different from God and that it can be the cause of all sorts of terrible things both personally and, in a measure, collectively. We have believed the body is separate and different from God and that it can be young or old, healthy or diseased, alive or dead. We have cut it open and explored what's inside, how it functions, and devised ten thousand treatments and procedures (and millions of textbook words justifying and explaining them) to repair it and extend its existence. All the while it is Awareness Itself in perfect order and beauty, requiring only our awareness of Awareness Itself to experience its truth.

So the first thing to realize is that all is not what it seems to be but is Awareness Itself. Everything we observe is God Itself or Awareness Itself. We observe people, bodies, things, shapes, colors, fragrances, and conditions which are all objective sensory experiences of the one infinity and omnipresence of Awareness. Nothing is actually physical, structural, material. There is no matter in awareness; there is just Awareness Itself, God, incorporeality.

Incorporeality was an immensely helpful word to me because it wipes out the belief in matter. If all is incorporeal, then obviously what I witness as my mind, body and world is incorporeal even though it appears to be corporeal. Well, that was a revelation to me, an immense help to me, and maybe to you too.

Awareness is all. Now pull back your awareness to the middle space again. *Feel* that body of awareness, that presence, that pure awareness unencumbered by things, people, conditions. Feel the release, the freedom you experience after having pulled back from names and definitions. This is your release from the earth and its good vs. bad belief.

(Spend a few moments in stillness, feeling the presence of Awareness Itself)

Release (pull away from), everything you are aware of. Feel and start living as Awareness Itself — indescribable Awareness Itself.

(Spend a few minutes in the stillness of the experience)

Now tell me, is there a limit to your awareness?

Was it born so many years ago, or is it simply *is?* Can it say much about itself, or would it simply say *I am* or *I am aware?*

Has this body of awareness, this middle space, a birth date? Does it have an age? Does it have a shape, a weight, a height, a color? Does it have aged skin or youthful skin? Is it good or bad? Can it talk back? Can it judge? Can it have an opinion? Does it contain matter that it has to deal with, that it has to maintain and protect, that it has to heal? Is any part of it poorer than another part? Does one part do battle with another part? Is there any part of it that lacks the whole? Is there a part of it that lives in a home and another part that is homeless? Is one part employed and another un-employed? Is one part hungry, unhappy, unfulfilled versus another part that is well-fed, happy, and fulfilled? Or is it simply a state of *is* devoid of name and definition, without good vs. bad?

My awareness simply *is.* I really cannot say much more about it other than that. What I *can* say is that *I am aware.* My awareness simply *is,* and that *is* is infinite.

Try to find the end of your awareness. Try to find the be-ginning of your awareness. Try to find the left or the right of it. Try to contain it. You are aware fully of the room in which you sit, but you are equally aware of outside the room. You can look through the window, and you discover that you are fully aware of the outside.

Nothing of your awareness is less than the whole of awareness being aware as and of this moment, this scene. The next moment, you may be aware of a different scene and it also will constitute the whole of awareness being aware as and of it. Because Awareness Itself is God, and be-cause God is eternally manifested, demonstrated, visible, tangible, and present right where you are, your awareness of this moment *is itself* the fullness of the kingdom of God, of good, of heaven as it is on earth.

At this moment, you are aware of me and the words I share with you on this page. Therefore, I and these words are *in* your awareness (they are certainly not outside of your awareness; if they were you could not be aware of them).

As you look into your room, is it not true that everything you observe, everything you sense (see, hear, taste, touch, smell) is *in* your awareness?

Now look out of the window and observe the farthest thing you possibly can, and realize that that thing is in your awareness. Whatever you are aware of exists in your awareness. *The whole universe is in your awareness.* You are not in the universe; the universe is in you.

I was walking a few nights ago and looked up into the sky and there was the tiniest sliver of the moon. I had to stop to gaze at the marvel of it and realize again that the whole sky with its billions of stars and tiny sliver of perfect moon exists in and as me and each individual. The moon is not "out there" a quarter of a million miles away; it and the infinity of space in which it seems to exist are all *in* us.

I am that I am. The whole of God is embodied in and as you, your consciousness, your awareness. The whole kingdom of heaven and earth and all the host of them are embodied, are fully manifested, demonstrated, visible, real, formed, tangible in and as your consciousness or awareness. All that you are aware *of* (and all that you ever can be aware of) is *in your* awareness, not outside of it, not separate from it.

The whole of God is embodied *in* and *as* your awareness. All is awareness. As you look at the moon, realize, That is awareness; it is a form of awareness. It is not a form of matter; there is no matter in awareness. It is a form of awareness. The trillions of stars are forms of awareness, forms of our very awareness, and we realize how beautiful our true identity is, how extraordinary are we — not personal we, but God we. How extraordinary, how magnificent, how miraculous are we!

The whole canopy of heaven exists in and as *our* awareness when we are aware of it. All the flowers on earth exist in and as our awareness. How miraculous are we! All the beings on earth exist in and as our awareness. All the birds and bird song on earth exist in and as our awareness; they are forms of us and our songs. How miraculous are we! All the mountains, all the valleys, all the streams, the rivers and the oceans exist in and as our awareness, *are* Awareness Itself.

All the youthfulness, all the beauty, all the vitality, all the joy, all the harmony of earth exist in and as *your* awareness and are Awareness Itself. How miraculous are we! All the life of earth, all the love of earth, all of heaven as earth (objectively sensed heaven), exist in and as your awareness.

I do not mean the life and love witnessed at this moment of time or in your human span of life; I mean *all* the life and *all* the love of earth, the eternity of earth, exist in and as your awareness. All the life you witness as people, animals, insects, trees, shrubs, flowers, grasses, oceans, streams, rivers, the breeze, the rain, the snow, the blue sky, the cloudy sky, the sunshine, the nighttime, the twinkling stars, the sounds, the fragrances — all this life *is* and exists *in* and *as your* awareness. It is Awareness Itself. All the money on earth (and infinitely more) exists in and as your awareness. It is Awareness Itself.

All of all that exists is in and as your awareness and is Awareness Itself. This is the truth of all. This is the nature, the character, the infinity, the omnipresence, the eternity of all. Awareness Itself is the key, not the way in which awareness appears to be to material sense, but Awareness Itself. Take little account of appearance. The key, the truth, the very presence, visibility, form and substance of truth, the very omnipresence of truth right here where you are is Awareness Itself.

This being true, tell me what you need. What is the one thing you need? Awareness Itself. Awareness Itself constitutes *all* that God is and has, all that good is and has. You do not need to seek the things of life because Awareness Itself constitutes all things. Once you have Awareness Itself, all the rest is included. All the good you could possibly need or want, even if you lived one million lifetimes on earth, comes free, is the free gift of God, the free gift of Awareness Itself when you *have* Awareness Itself, when you *live by* Awareness Itself, when you seek nothing of what appears to be, but seek the kingdom of Awareness Itself. "Seek not the things of life." Do not seek anything for your life, for your love, for your finances, for your business, for your neighborhood, for your family. Do not seek the things, but "seek the kingdom of God instead and then all the *things* are added unto you" — added unto your awareness. Not only are they added, but "it is the Father's good pleasure to give you the kingdom." It is the good pleasure of Awareness Itself to give you the infinity, the omnipresence and the very tangible form and visibility of all good, as you do just one thing — know that Awareness Itself is all, and then seek only Awareness Itself, knowing that it itself constitutes the very form and visibility, the very presence of all and unconditional good.

If we seek the objects and conditions of awareness in themselves, we have taken our sense out of Awareness Itself and now will not experience the things. We have re-attached our awareness to the world; we're bound to the world. As soon as we attach to something we can name and describe, we've bound ourselves again to the world and therefore have bound heaven.

However, as you pull back and again become aware of

Awareness Itself, this middle place, this seeming emptiness between you and a person or you and it (you and the world, you and what seems to be), you are instantly back in Awareness Itself. You've unencumbered yourself; you've released yourself from the world again. Therefore, you have released heaven, and as you now seek only Awareness Itself — an ever greater *living* experience of Awareness Itself — you will quickly discover that Awareness Itself constitutes all good. Good quickly reveals itself where bad appeared to be — illness or even disease, lack, limitation, hate, insufficiency, homelessness, poverty, unhappiness.

Bad dissolves and good becomes evident, real, visible, by your being wholeheartedly attentive to, seeking, loving Awareness Itself. "Love the Lord thy God with all your heart and all your soul and all your mind and all your strength." Love Awareness Itself with all your heart and all your soul and all your mind and all your strength.

It is easy to fall in love with Awareness Itself because as we pull away from that which seems to be, and abide here in this middle space, beginning to *feel* it, how quickly we are unburdened, unencumbered and free. How quickly we feel the freedom, the release in that which truly is! Yes, it is easy to fall in love with Awareness Itself. Who does not want to live unencumbered, free, released, knowing that this very experience is heaven released on earth as individual you and me?

Never again seek a person, a thing, a condition, a place, an amount. Never do it; never again seek to experience a nicer, more loving, more gentle person; and never seek to be rid of a nasty one. Do not seek to be released from the prison of disease, of lack and limitation, of injustice or immorality. Do not seek to be released from any hardship or even pain. You will fail. I can tell you that because I was a master at failing in this. We cannot be free *of* a thing; we can only be free *in* Awareness Itself. Then we have nothing left to be free of.[1]

Of course, the Master has told us, Do not seek things (do not seek the good and do not seek to be rid of the bad), but seek the kingdom of God instead. Seek the totality of Awareness Itself instead, and then all the good things, the true good, spring up and fill your life, spring up in your body, your mind, your family, your neighborhood, your business, and the far side of your world. All that is becomes evident as the joy, harmony, peace and fulfillment of you.

However, if we once fall back into the trap of seeking the *things,* the *conditions,* the *hims* and the *hers,* then we'll have to get along with the finiteness we sought. Unfortunately, that includes both the good and the bad. We cannot be free of good and bad *until* the moment we free ourselves by *being* Awareness Itself.

We bind ourselves. Nothing binds us. We are not stuck in a world of good and bad. We are not stuck with disease, lack, limitation, hate, immorality or homelessness. Let us hear it closely — we are never stuck with anything bad. *We* are attaching our experience *to it* by believing it.

Because bad is never stuck to us, we can instantly release the experience of it by lifting into Awareness Itself.

Watch how quickly disease dissolves when we pay it no more attention, release our concern about it, and lift into and live in and by Awareness Itself. The very act of releasing that which we are concerned about in Awareness Itself releases heaven. Now disease has nothing more to do with us.

---

[1] Editor's note: We cannot be free *of* a thing because belief cannot free itself of itself. If we believe we need to be free of a thing, then we are the believer, the belief itself, the thing we need to be freed from! When we are aware that we are Awareness Itself and that Awareness Itself is all, then there is no one needing to be free and nothing to be free of.

We may still have pain or some kind of limitation in our body for awhile, but from the moment of release the trouble is over and quickly on its way out of our awareness.

Watch how quickly even what's called fatal disease dissolves. It instantly loses its power and activity, its effect. Any untrue form, any activity is made impotent the instant *we* release our sense from it and come here to this middle place, come here to Awareness Itself.

There is no magic to it; there is no special condition to being aware of Awareness Itself. Just be aware of Awareness Itself by releasing yourself from the things, the people, the conditions. Pull back and become aware of the middle space, and then rest and freely receive.

Feel the freedom; feel that inability to describe Awareness Itself. That inability is the freedom. Feel the joy, the peace, the spaciousness of it; feel the unencumbered self, and abide there.

Seek Awareness Itself alone and experience *I* abiding in you as the feeling of peace, of presence, of light or warmth or love far more palpably, far more alive in you, living you.

Be assured that as you pay no more attention to the things of life in themselves — good or bad — and give all or as much of your sincere attention as you can to Awareness Itself, your whole life transforms. Disease, lack, limitation, suffering, pain are quickly proven to be nothing of their own selves (just belief), and health and harmony prevail when you live and move and have your being in Awareness Itself.

This is the most practical way of everyday life. Go out and live it. Live it for even a full day and see what begins to take place. Good becomes infallibly apparent because belief is not an entity. It cannot resist truth. Nothing in heaven or earth can resist the evidence, the actual form and visibility of truth because nothing but truth exists.

This is why, when we release belief, release the things of

the world, our very act of doing so releases heaven. The moment heaven is released in us, we see clearly that which before, in our bound state, we could not see. Nothing is hidden in the mind of God. When God fills our awareness and we live by Awareness Itself, every good person, thing and condition becomes visible and tangible right where we are.

This soon proves itself in your experience as you do your best to maintain your attention on Awareness Itself, to seek Awareness Itself, not the people, not the things, not the conditions, not the seemingly logical solutions to life's problems. In fact, logic turns out to be most illogical because it is of the intellect. Logic is based on sense testimony which is nothing of its own self. So logic based on sense testimony is no logic at all.

CHAPTER FOUR

AWARENESS IS AWARE
OF ITSELF ALONE
(ALL THAT GOD IS AND HAS)

Awareness Itself constitutes all that God is and has. It is the very substance, activity, form, visibility, tangibility, and presence of good. Awareness Itself, the finished kingdom of good, does not evolve, change, or move. Awareness Itself already *is*.

We move our *sense* of awareness. We can move our sense anywhere we wish to throughout our universe. We are and have the freedom of sense and that which is back of sense (God, Awareness Itself). The minute we attach sense to sensed *things* we are the prodigal being. We have taken our tangible experience out of the kingdom of good. We have fallen for the hypnotic suggestion of collective belief, and now everything of our experience is personal, finite, local, and of the universe of good and bad.

Awareness Itself Remains the Same

Our sense of awareness does not change Awareness Itself. Awareness Itself is infinite and omnipresent, even though our moment-by-moment sense is usually (until we awaken) personal, finite, local, and particular. Nevertheless, the awareness we are — the *I* of us, the *object* of awareness, and the awareness we are aware *with* — is (all) the one infinity and omnipresence of Awareness Itself.

Realize the infinity and omnipresence of awareness. As you remain detached from the *things* of life in themselves, and gently maintain the realization of the infinity and omnipresence of awareness, seeking nothing else, the harmony and limitlessness of people, things and conditions come forth in sense. Intellectual knowledge (the *letter* of truth) alone is insufficient to evidence God; *realization* reveals the fruits of good.

Turn your awareness to a particular place in your room. At first, your awareness will be of the *things* that populate that area of your room. Now gently defocus from the things, into a sense of Awareness Itself, the *substance* of the things. Feel Awareness Itself, relax in it, bathe in it, let go of the sense of "personal you." Begin to let Awareness Itself "take over," fill you, and live itself freely in and as you. Even within a minute or two you begin to have a greater realization and feeling of the limitlessness of Awareness Itself which fills your senses. The *feeling,* the *sense,* is the presence experienced.

No Boundary

Awareness is not fixed; it is not bound. No person, thing, activity, amount, condition, or place can limit it, imprison it, bind it. "What hinders you? . . . Rise, take up thy bed, and walk." (Galatians 5:7; John 5:8)

Awareness Itself is omnipresent.

Awareness Itself is God Itself. Of course, nothing hinders God. God *is*. Therefore, nothing hinders you or me when we live yielded to Awareness Itself, letting *it be* and *see* and *reveal* the way "for us."

As you are aware of Awareness Itself, realize the infinity, the omnipresence, the eternity, the kingdom of God it is. Realize that it itself constitutes all that God is and has, all the reality, all the substance, all the form, all the visibility that God is and has: all the true good, all the everlasting good, all the wisdom, all the omniscience, all the *now* experience.

Now become aware of another thing in your room while staying as Awareness Itself, staying in between what seems to be you and the "outer" objectivity of people, things, conditions, faces.

Everything true about the previous point of awareness, is true of this new point of your awareness. You have simply moved your awareness; therefore you have moved that which constitutes all that God is and has in your experience. You've moved it around your experience or to a new point of your experience. Now move it to another new point of your experience. Make sure you're not thinking of things or people or conditions. Stay in Awareness Itself.

Wherever You Look, There *I Am*

Wherever you look, there is all that God is and has. The whole kingdom of God is embodied in and is Awareness Itself which is aware as individual you, me and all.

There is no such thing as intangible God or heaven or truth; there is no such thing as invisible God, unreal, impractical God or truth or awareness. So as you remain aware of Awareness Itself — the substance or the presence of awareness, that which you are aware *as* and *with* — you keep yourself seated in the kingdom of God which itself constitutes all the good form, substance, visibility, place, amount, mind, body, and purpose fulfilled that God is and has.

You can be aware one inch from your nose or of the farthest object or scene in your universe. They are the same thing as long as you stay open and attentive to Awareness Itself rather than to the sensed pictures, the *things*. You will never be *unaware* of the things, but as long as you do not *attach* to them but stay aware of Awareness Itself, then you are in the kingdom of God, in God consciousness. You have nothing to describe, nothing to hold onto, nothing to need or desire from Awareness Itself. Awareness Itself *is all*. That which appears to be, is not that which *is*. That which appears to be is an objective sense of that which *is,* which is awareness, is infinite, omnipresent, borderless, uncontainable, unnameable, unconditional.

Awareness is all; therefore, what is sensed as the physical body is not a physical body but is a body of awareness. It is a body of awareness within and without, the body of Awareness Itself. No cell of matter exists there, no physical organ or function; there are no skin, no brain, no eyes, no other physical sense faculties.

Realize —

I am the body of Awareness; my body is a body of my awareness.

Do not try to equate it to the physical. Fill yourself with Awareness Itself and be satisfied with the experience of Awareness alone. Nothing exists except Awareness.

I am a body of Awareness and because I am, I am all that God is and has because God is Awareness Itself.

Moving Your Sense of Awareness Around

Move your awareness into the center of your body, but maintain Awareness Itself rather than attaching your sense to organs or functions of the body. You are not attempting to be aware of a physical center of the body; you are not attempting to become aware of the "truth" of a physical body. There isn't any. You are aware of Awareness Itself *as* the body.

I am the body of awareness and besides awareness, there is nothing else about me.

I am not aware of; *I am aware* as. *I am aware as a body of Awareness Itself.*

Therefore what am I? What is my body? It is the infinitude; it is the omnipresence, the entire kingdom of God; it is the entire creation; it is the entirety of eternity itself. Eternity does not exist anywhere except as your body of awareness. If you believe it does exist somewhere else, then you're believing that there is existence outside of your awareness and that isn't true.

(A few minutes of silence)

Are you aware of Awareness Itself? Do you feel your body as awareness? Do you feel even a little released from the physical? Do you feel a bit freer as the body of awareness? Then you are. Always remember that what may seem to be a tiny amount of Awareness Itself is actually the whole because you cannot have a portion. God is infinite, omnipresent, indivisible. We can be *aware of* only a small portion, but actually what we are aware of is the entirety.

We are awakening from a deep sleep. We may, for awhile, feel only a "little" of the presence of Awareness Itself. Being *aware* of a little does not mean we *have* only a little. Hear it. As soon as we are even a tiny amount aware of Awareness Itself, we have the whole kingdom. The woman only had to touch the hem of the Master's clothing to be released from a lifetime of disease, not throw her arms around him and hold him to herself. Just the touch of the hem was enough for the entire healing, the whole kingdom to be evident. So if you are touching the hem of Awareness Itself, you have the whole of the kingdom this instant — visible, tangible, real, evident. It is done; it is complete. Your demonstration is complete; your manifested good is visible and real.

Now, how does your body feel? It feels good, doesn't it? It feels freer, feels healthier; it *is*. It feels more eternal; it *is*.

(A few moments of silence)

Now move your awareness back into the space in between – somewhere between you and that which seems to be. Choose an object to focus on and become aware of the center of the object, the substance rather than the apparent solid form of it. Remain in and as Awareness Itself. Realize that the object appears to have solid form, shape, size, color, and location but these are images alone. What it truly is, is Awareness Itself. There is nothing more or less about it.

(A few minutes of pondering and feeling the object's body of awareness)

What do you begin to sense about the object? Is it even a little different to you now compared to how it seemed when you observed it merely as a material object? Oh, yes it is. If it is Awareness Itself, which it is, what is its nature? What is its character? Is it finite or infinite? Is it local or omnipresent? Is it simply what it appears to be, or is it infinitely greater than its outer appearance?

This is your work every hour: As you observe an object, know it and feel it as Awareness Itself. Dismiss the way it appears to be (still seeing it, but dismissing the belief in its independent reality), keeping your awareness as Awareness Itself, as your only real interest, the only important aspect of this experience, the only thing you truly seek, the only actual entity, the only thing you want to know more about.

Never attempt to equate Awareness Itself to an object; do not attempt to link them. The object is merely sense imagery. It has no meaning in and of its own self; there is no correlation between it and any other imagery, any other form. It is a solo image of sense. That is all. It is entity-less, substance-less, form-less in itself. It has no power, no presence in itself. It has no character, no nature, no faculty, no use in itself. It seems to have these qualities, but judge not by the appearance. What we're interested in is truth.

We can still use the object as it's useful in sensory experience, but we are now aware of it as a body of Awareness Itself, and so we learn to be aware of our objective sense, our world, as it appears to be, but never attach to it, never seek anything for it of its own self, realizing that the truth of the it of it is Awareness Itself, God itself, the kingdom of God itself.

By seeking only Awareness Itself, seeking to remain in Awareness Itself, we have access to the kingdom of God — visible, real, palpable — *as* this object, and as all objectivity.

As you continue to observe your chosen object, see it, but do not see it; use it but do not use it. Do you see? Have it in your experience, but far more, have Awareness Itself filling you.

I am in the world, but not of it. I am in the object, but not of it. I am of Awareness Itself and the object is in my awareness.

*My body is in my awareness; loved one, family, friends, students,
the whole population, are in my awareness; money is in my awareness; my business is in my awareness; all its detail is in my awareness
but I am not of them. I am, and am of, Awareness Itself.*

I'll tell you a great secret about awareness. *Awareness is
and can only be aware of itself.* We have heard this truth in many
ways: Only God is; therefore only God *can.* Only God sees
itself. Only truth sees itself. Only spirit sees itself. Realize
this regarding Awareness. *Awareness is only aware of itself.*

The reason is that only Awareness is; only God is; nothing else exists, but it is fascinating and important to realize
that Awareness sees only, and can see only, itself.

Now observe an expanse of your awareness — people,
objects, places, amounts, colors, fragrances, weights, sizes,
positions. Awareness can only be aware of itself, so what
constitutes this expanse of your awareness? It is all Awareness Itself.

Nothing exists except Awareness Itself. What appears to
be matter, isn't; it is awareness. What appear to be various
materials, aren't; they are awareness. We may observe or be
working with fabric, wood, metal, plaster, paint, color, fragrance, sound, flesh; we have what appears to be a mental
mind thinking about and detecting a material world; we have
what appears to be the physical body consisting of physical
organs and functions. None of this is true. Awareness is, and
can be aware only of itself.

All is Awareness Itself. Everything we are aware of is
Awareness Itself. And because Awareness Itself is infinity,
all is infinite. Awareness Itself is God; therefore all is and
has the quality, nature and characteristic of God — infinity,
omnipresence, eternity, perfection, the finished kingdom,
unconditional good, the same yesterday, today, and forever.
Truth becomes evident in the most real and practical way

because it is the only actuality. It becomes evident by the degree that we are filled with this truth, by the degree that we live this truth, by the degree that Awareness Itself is living us, is being and seeing itself for us, which is then sensed as the objective forms of good.

Our sole role in experience is one-pointed: to seek the kingdom of God itself, to seek Awareness Itself *as itself, for itself.* That's it, and the reason that is all we are required to do is because Awareness Itself *constitutes* all that God is and has. So when we seek and are satisfied with Awareness Itself, we discover that Awareness Itself pours through our uncluttered senses being its own image and likeness *for* us. We're not involved; we're not assistants to God. We have heard this in practically every Miracle Self book and class. It is time to take it literally: He performs that which we are given to do. It is the Father's good pleasure to give us the kingdom. The finished kingdom is inside you and it is outside you.

No "place" of your awareness is anything other than the full kingdom of good, but the only way of seeing it, of having it, of having the real experience is by seeking Awareness Itself, by being satisfied with the experience of Awareness Itself, not wandering off trying to equate Awareness Itself to humanity, objectivity, physicality, materiality. Do not do it. Awareness is only aware of itself. What *appears to be* the universe, *appears to be* humanity, the physical body, the material, objective world, isn't; it is Awareness Itself.

As we seek Awareness Itself, as we feel the presence of Awareness Itself alive in us, then along with Saint Paul we can say, I live, yet not I (not I, the personal sense of self), Awareness Itself lives me.

No matter *where* you are aware, no matter what you are aware *of* (which you now know is all Awareness Itself), it is your individual experience of awareness. Can you separate and divide your awareness? Can you take a scalpel and slice your awareness into two, move the two parts away from each other, so that you now have separate, divided awareness? No. Awareness is one and indivisible. Awareness is omnipresence, "closer than breathing, nearer than hands and feet."

I and awareness are one. I and awareness are synonyms. All is awareness; therefore I and all are one, indivisible, inseparable. Right here where I am, the infinity and omnipresence of awareness are. The awareness I am aware *with* constitutes, *is,* the entirety of the kingdom of God, good.

The whole universe, the whole of the infinitude, exists in and as my awareness. Therefore, I am and I have *all* that infinity is and has right here where I am, and right where (anywhere) I place my awareness. As we heard in Stand on Truth all those years ago, *Wherever you look, there I am.* You see more clearly what that means now.

And because Awareness Itself is and is fully visible as itself as all, when you yield your sense of awareness including your sense of the person or thing you are aware *of,* Awareness Itself is free in you to reveal itself as that which you observe. You now see clearly, and all is good.

You as you know yourself to be, and the world as you know it to be, do not disappear from awareness as you yield and let Awareness Itself take over. You and your world are revealed as their glorious and purposeful all-good reality. Earth as it is in heaven is opened to sense as we give our sense of awareness to that which it is in truth, Awareness Itself.

Give your I to *I* itself, give your being to *being* itself and then behold your fields of awareness yield abundant crops of good.

As we continually seek Awareness Itself and the experience of Awareness Itself, as our main purpose each day is to *feel* that presence, then wherever we look, whomever or whatever we observe is infallibly, tangibly evident as greater degrees of life, love, harmony and abundance. We are not interested in appearance, nor do we believe it or judge it. We are interested in Awareness Itself — the faculty of clear seeing.

As we ourselves maintain our awareness in Awareness Itself and continually yield to it, that *itself* is the faculty of truthful vision. We have no other effort to make, in truth, other than the one effort of keeping our awareness in Awareness Itself. The "rest" is automatic and infallible.

Seek the kingdom of God and all the *things* will be added. We do not have to go out there to get them, demonstrate them; we do not have to think about (take concern for) them, or mentally or materially manipulate the pairs of opposites to attain the good *things* we believe we need or desire. God constitutes all good, so when we have God, all the good things of earth are included. We are not involved. We already *are* and *have* the kingdom of our perfect good right here where we are, whether in the so-called body or out of it, whether in here or out there. *I am* that I am. The one thing we must do is let God be God as God *is,* in and through us. Then we discover that all the truth of truths becomes real and practical in our everyday experience.

We have been unable to *see* the infinity we are and have because we've been looking at, believing and seeking, the objects of awareness instead of Awareness Itself. We have sought good for that which appears to be; sought health or healing for what we have believed is the physical body; sought material good to solve material bad; sought to achieve or attain the good things and conditions of love, success, financial stability or even wealth, peace. Well, we cannot find what we have been seeking. All these experiences and an infinity more already exist. All we need do is wake up to and *be* what they are. Nothing of health is missing; nothing of love is missing; nothing of wealth is missing; nothing of harmony is missing; nothing of fulfilled purpose is missing. I am that I am. I only have to *awaken* to that which I eternally am and have. The way of it is to seek the kingdom of God and then "all these *things* will be added unto you". That which we were previously unaware of now fills our awareness. We wake up. Our eyes are opened.

"Whereas I was blind, now I see." My eyes are open. Awareness is seeing for me. The fog has dissipated. I am released and free. I am as limitless as Awareness Itself because I am Awareness Itself.

The world is yours; the entire objective sense of good without limit, without condition, is yours. There is no limit to any good, any category or place or amount, any form of immediate, visible good. The only limit is our own sense of limit brought about by our not abiding in Awareness Itself and having Awareness Itself abide in us; by attaching to that which seems to be – the human, the physical, the material, the objective. The entire world of good without limit is you and yours. *I and awareness are one. I and the Father are one. I and truth are one.*

As quickly as you can become aware of and live by Awareness Itself is how quickly your good is visibly with you because Awareness Itself *is the good,* fully formed, fully visible, fully real, fully practical.

Make sure you understand. We do not go to Awareness Itself to get objective good. Awareness Itself *is,* Awareness Itself constitutes all that good is, all that God is and has. Awareness Itself *is the good.* Our experience of Awareness Itself is our tangible experience of good. As we live and move and have our being in and as Awareness Itself, as we feel Awareness Itself living us more fully every day, the objective sense of it becomes evident. In other words, more good constantly flows and is evident throughout our experience.

CHAPTER FIVE

AWARENESS KNOWS

One statement of truth that I had great difficulty with (and, of course, many tend to) is the beautiful and promising yet confusing Luke 12:30 — "Your Father knows that you have need of these things". If he truly does, why is he not giving them to me?

If God, which is spirit, has no humanity in it, no mentality in it, nothing physical in it, nothing of matter in it — yet we obviously need the good of these things to live satisfactorily on earth — how is it that the Father knows what we have need of?

God is the infinitude, boundless all of all, and God is incorporeal. Therefore all of all is incorporeal, yet I need what I believe is corporeal good because I am, my body is, and everything of my world is to my sense corporeal. How then can it be true that the Father knows what I have need of and that it is his good pleasure to give it to me? I haven't seen much sign of his good pleasure giving it to me, so how can this promise be true?

Well, it is true, but we have to understand how and why it is. Always remember, God or truth can only do for us what it can do through us. If our awareness is foggy or dull with belief, with personal self need or desire, if there is an aspect of truth that hasn't yet registered within, these act as blocks, disguising the omnipresence of good from our tangible sense.

Everything of existence is *in here — in and as awareness.* Nothing of existence is *out there,* not even one breath or thought away. Remember the poet: "Closer is he than breathing, and nearer than hands and feet." All that exists is closer to you than your very breath, closer than sense. This, the deep within and solitude of being, is where we do our truth work. If we believe we can do any work in the outer, or by considering the outer, we are mistaken. We have gone too far out from where truth is — the "secret place of the most high [the most within and pure]".

From the deep within, let us hear clarity around this so that you may see that which is.

All is God — Awareness Itself, consciousness, incorporeality, infinity, omnipresence, omniscience, omnipotence, *I, I am.* Let us mainly use Awareness Itself.

All is Awareness Itself. Awareness Itself sees only itself. It does not see a belief about it, a concept of it, a perception or misperception about it. It does not see good and bad (which are opposite extremes of belief). Therefore, the multitudinous forms we observe — persons, bodies, activities, amounts, places; everything we see, hear, taste, touch, smell and think — are, despite appearance, Awareness Itself. All is the body of awareness. Wherever you look, there *I am* because nothing but *I* exists.

Nothing about appearance is untruthful as long as nothing is believed about it. As long as we exist in and as Awareness Itself, appearance is of the nature, character and quality of Awareness Itself — infinite, omnipresent, unconditional good. We exist without a personal sense of self, without idea, without need or desire, without attachment. We realize that everything everywhere is *is*. We cannot name and define *is* and we do not wish to try. All *is;* names, definitions and attachments are unnecessary. We know that the only thing that presents itself to us is *is*. No other power, presence, or form exists. *Is* presents itself to us because *is* is the only presence.

The pictures of *is,* the three-dimensional images, have no meaning in themselves, have no consequence in themselves, have no correlation to anything else *in themselves.* Your and my appearances in themselves (as personal-appearing selves) are nothing, are meaningless, powerless, substance-less, formless, principle-less. We have no power, no faculty, no purpose in and of our own selves. The one and only quality, meaning and purpose we have is as beings of *God-is.*

When we know this truth there is no need to believe anything about each other and no need to do anything for each other based on belief and appearance. We ignore appearance and accept the images of each other, no matter what they suggest, good or bad, as *is.* As your image of being and body presents itself to me it does not, in itself, mean anything. It is just an *is* in my experience. Who you truly are, is what matters and reveals itself to me when I know that you are the presence of God appearing as individual being, when I know that you, as true identity, are *I* or *I am,* "the Christ, the Son of [the individual objective sense of] the living God".

You are divine being presenting itself to me. Now every time I catch sight of you, even on the outer reaches of my peripheral awareness, you are a divine appointment to me, and I am to you because we both know that nothing except

God presents itself to us. Even one minute with you is a divine appointment because nothing separate or less than the presence of God is taking place. Nothing else *ever* takes place because nothing except God *is*.

In a human state of existence, when we observe a flower, a tree, a person, it could either be of no particular interest or love to us, or of much interest and love. If we happen to know and love the flower, the tree, the person, we have a very different reaction to seeing it, him, or her than we do if we do not know or care for it, him, or her. This variable alone demonstrates the non-entity, the non-quality of the forms (sensed images) in themselves. They are *believed* to be entities in and of their own selves; therefore they can only bring up a good vs. bad response in the believer.

In a spiritual state of existence, on the other hand, we realize that all is the presence of God appearing to us as person, thing and condition. Therefore, all has the same value and quality to us. We sense *through* the outer-appearing form to the presence within. That presence is immortal, eternal, the tangible presence of God itself. Our previous human disinterest vs. interest softens and gradually dissolves, and our spiritual recognition and God-love for all emerges.

All is awareness within and without. Awareness is Awareness Itself or spirit. All the people, things, places, activities, circumstances and conditions (our objective senses) that constitute the universe are forms of awareness, not forms of matter. This is the key to the tangible God experience. Nothing except awareness is, and awareness has no matter in it whatsoever; therefore all form is the form of awareness. Mind is the faculty of awareness, bodies are bodies of awareness, objects are objectively sensed awareness. What appears to be corporeal isn't; all is incorporeal. What appears to be flesh, isn't; it is a form of awareness. What appears to be matter (and all the forms, the structures of matter) isn't;

it is our material sense of that which is one hundred percent awareness. Awareness sees itself alone (because nothing except awareness exists). That which we are aware *of* is Awareness Itself.

Awareness Expanding

Because existence is infinite, we experience an infinite variety of seemingly different beings, bodies, materials, structures, places, circumstances. Our awareness is ever opening and expanding into the infinity of Awareness Itself. The expansion of awareness is witnessed as what appears to be an increase in the population and great industry advancements. There is no actual population increase or industry advancements. God is infinite individual being, faculty and function and as our awareness of infinity expands, we see it as greater "amounts" of improvement and fulfillment. "As I be lifted up I draw all men [material sense] unto me." (John 12:32) Each degree of expanded awareness witnesses itself as greater good form, faculty and function.

Buckminster Fuller's "Knowledge Doubling Curve" states that until 1900 human knowledge doubled approximately every century. By the end of World War II, knowledge was doubling every twenty-five years. Today, different categories of knowledge have different rates of growth. Nanotechnology knowledge is doubling every two years; clinical knowledge is doubling every eighteen months. On average human knowledge is doubling every thirteen months, and IBM research predicts that human knowledge will soon double every twelve hours.

This represents the speed at which collective human awareness is awakening. Most are unaware of what is taking place; they simply accept and enjoy the benefits of the outer forms of expanded awareness. Those of us who are awakening to true identity have clearer understanding and therefore recognize and value the outer forms for what they truly are: God or Awareness Itself.

"Know the truth, and the truth will make you free." Almost every person is aware of great human, industry and world innovation; however, those *who do not know the truth* continue to exist in belief, experiencing the pairs of opposites. For them, great advancement and innovation sit side by side with greater pain and suffering. They suffer all the ills, diseases, stress, accidents, hardships, aversion, immorality and injustice that the rest of the population does. However, by the degree you and I maintain our awareness in and live by Awareness Itself, we are largely free of and immune to the pairs of opposites, in God.

We eventually, by the degree of our attained purity of Awareness Itself, bypass the need for agencies of fulfillment. Living as and by Awareness Itself is the direct experience of oneness with all good. The *I* of us *is life itself;* we do not need agencies of life in the forms of drugs, manipulations or procedures. The *I* of us *is infinity itself;* we do not need the agencies of money, business, investment in order to evidence an infinity of wealth. The *I* of us *is love itself;* we do not need to find the right partner and learn effective love techniques in order to experience the fulfillment of love and relationship. I am that I am. It is my purpose, as realized *I,* to *give* to my world, not to get; to be the life, the supply, the love and the light of the world, not to go in search of these for personal fulfillment. "I am come that they might have life, and that they might have it more abundantly." (John 10:10)

We each must ever more recognize *I* as true identity and yield to it. Day by day, we awaken more to that which *is* and live by its principles. Our eyes are more opened, and as they are, we discover our lives filled with a greater degree of good — the one true life, self-contained, self-complete, ever-present, invariable, undamageable, unchangeable, unaffectable. *Is* does not, of course, require an agency of support or fulfillment. *Is is* — eternally self-embodied, active and purposeful. As we become attuned and live by Awareness Itself our lives are transformed. We become empty of self and its human and material reliances, and find ourselves animated and fulfilled as the self-embodiment, activity and purpose of is. One by one, the agencies of good we relied upon drop away until we are free in Awareness Itself.

We live in the world but are not of it. We no longer want or need worldly things in themselves. We *are* and *have* Awareness Itself living us — the infinite and omnipresent all good already established, demonstrated, manifested and visible within and without. Awareness *is* and sees itself "for us." As we release the desire and believed need for worldly things in themselves, only God remains in us, and we discover that with God alone, the infinity of God-*things* is included. God *constitutes* the objective sense of itself. "The kingdom of God is inside you and it is outside you." God sense is automatic and infallible when we leave it itself to *be.* We do not require an agency to give us the true image and likeness; the image and likeness is already present, and now we see it clearly.

Body

Your body is the one healthy and vital body. Through objective sense it appears to be physical, and it remains so for as long as we exist at the "this world" level of awareness. The objective sense of the body devoid of belief is true and beautiful and reveals itself to be so. Belief suggests that the body is exposed to both good and bad influence, that the body can be healthy, vital and youthful and can also fall victim to accident, injury, disease or old age. Belief is itself separateness and difference from God, and so when our awareness is imbued with belief, we are filled with the suggestion that the body is a physical entity, not only separate from God but also from every other body on earth. Tens of thousands of industries have emerged to support the physical body to make the best of its health, fitness and beauty and to sooth or heal its infirmities, diseases and old age.

The spiritual body *is* and is not in need of anything. It *is* life itself, eternity itself, perfection itself. It is full bodily purpose and fulfillment. "I am the life of the world." *I* am. Realize this of your *I,* your Awareness Itself.

The very *I* I am *is* the life of the world. This realization and experience is, if you like, the true "agency" — the realization of *I* being given to the world. That is the agency, the lotion, the pill, the procedure. You can give spiritual "lotions, pills and procedures" to your world each and every day, and you should do. This is casting the bread upon the waters and watching it come back to you thirtyfold, sixtyfold, a hundredfold.

Cast thy bread — thy spiritual awareness, the true agency of good, the realization that *I am the life of the world* — onto the waters of awareness. Then watch the miracles of life, the miracles of healing, come back abundantly and free as the constituents of Awareness Itself, and, most profoundly, they are free to all who receive them. How much does it cost a person to receive your truthful agency, your spiritual lotion, pill, procedure, your conscious realization that all is life itself? It is free for all people who touch your awareness. It is the gift of God expressing through you.

The image you see of me and my body is actually the image and likeness of God despite the good or bad appearance belief tints it to be. In your *conscious* realization of life itself being all that exists, you know that what presents itself to you as the form of me is Awareness Itself as individual being. This conscious realization quickly heals me, by the degree of my receptivity. If I am unreceptive, your realization still witnesses my health and wholeness, but I might not sense it. My open or closed sense does not affect you and your demonstration. *You* have realized it and evidenced it within, and that's the one thing that matters.

It Is the Father's Good Pleasure to Give You the Kingdom

Omniscience *knows*. You do not have to know; I do not have to know; even the Master does not have to know. We of our own selves *cannot* know. "I of my own self can do nothing. It is the Father within me that does these works", not I myself. Do not look to me. (John 5:30, John 14:10) "Truly, I say to you that the Son can do nothing of his own accord, except what he sees the Father doing; for the things which the Father does, the same the Son does also." (John 5:19)

Bring to mind the fact that only awareness exists. What is awareness? Incorporeal or corporeal? Of course, awareness is incorporeal. Therefore, what is its nature? Is it infinite or finite, local or universal? Is it temporal or everlasting, matter or spirit, human or divine? We know the answers. *All* is Awareness Itself — *all, all!*

All *without exception,* no matter how we describe it, what we believe it to be, whether we believe it is within but not without, is the omnipresence of God. *All* is the omnipresence of Awareness Itself. Nothing exists except Awareness Itself "and the fullness thereof". All that exists is and is fully evident to Awareness as it itself is.

The forms of awareness have unfortunately been labeled human, mental, physical, material; all is believed to exist as a result of cause and effect; all is believed to exist in time and occupy a certain amount of space in the universe. And all is entirely incorrect. The *truth* is that all is Awareness It-self which has no label, which is infinity and omnipresence, which is not the result of cause or the form of effect, which is timeless and spaceless.

We are, and are aware of bodies of awareness. Look into your room again and remind yourself of this truth. We do not see human beings with fleshy bodies, we are not mate-rially aware, we do not think mental thoughts with a mental mind. There *isn't* one, so how could it think mental thoughts? There isn't a physical body, so how could we ex-perience physical conditions? There isn't a material world constituting material substances and forms, so how could we experience these? There isn't structure, size, shape, weight, color, fragrance. There is only Awareness Itself.

Knowing this, what explains our objective experience of Awareness Itself in which all these nuances of appearance seem to be real?

Awareness Itself is all; therefore mind is Awareness Itself. The mind is simply our current level of awareness — one of the "many mansions in my Father's house", one of the infi-nite degrees of awareness. And because this level of aware-ness is objective, we have objective sense.

Because all of existence is oneness, mind (sense) *is* form. We do not sense separate form existing "out there"; sense it-self is form - mind *is* form; form *is* mind. What we call *mind* is our avenue of awareness, and because awareness is infinite, the forms of our universe are infinite in variety, nature, and quality. It is for this reason that the infinity of universal form appears to us as having three-dimensions and endless local-ities, sizes, shapes, weights, colors and purposes.

When the infinity of universal form is devoid of our be-lief about it, it is witnessed as being true, boundless, divinely purposeful and forever fulfilling. Belief plunges our expe-rience into pairs of opposites, and now we find our experience in a constant battle with itself — the battle between good and bad (God and evil). When it is realized that the mind is not a power that diminishes God, changes God, separates God but is the very presence of God simply objectively sensed, then form is free in us to appear and act God-like.

This is the key to what has been called healing, harmony, peace, prosperity, love. This is the whole key. The objective, three-dimensional, sense of God that we call "this world" is actually Awareness Itself, heaven itself. "This world" is a misleading term. If we believe "this world" exists, then we must also believe another world called "that world" or "heaven" exists. No. Only one world exists. What is true of heaven is true of earth. What God does in heaven, God does in earth because heaven and earth are one. "The place whereon you stand is holy ground." It would be better to omit every word and phrase except God or I Am. All is God. I live and move and have my being in the infinite ocean of God, of Awareness Itself. Our earthly existence is a wondrous, divinely purposeful experience of the only existence there is — which is God — which happens to be at this level of our awareness three-dimensional. But our three-dimensional sense has not changed God in the slightest.

As I see you, I see God. As I see all that constitutes my environment this hour, *I see God* because there is no other existence to see. "If you see me, you see the Father who sent me." The word "sent" is easily misunderstood. It means *is* this presence, *is* this form you see as me, the man or the woman. The Master is saying that if you see me, if you see this seeming human being performing miraculous feats, it is not a man in possession of super powers, wielding them through a material world. You are seeing true identity — individual God being — in a high state of realization revealing truth. Realize that you (and every person regardless of realization) see the presence of Awareness Itself or God itself no matter whether that presence seems to be human, animal, vegetable, mineral, animate or inanimate.

No matter what you observe, what you experience, whether seemingly good or bad, it is Awareness Itself, the very presence of God itself.

Awareness is incorporeal even though it *seems,* to sense, to be corporeal. *There is no corporeality.* Corporality is nothing more than sense. In this realization lies the entire key to understanding how the Father knows what we have need of, and why it is his good pleasure to give it to us. All is incorporeal. Spiritual realization illumines our incorporeal awareness. Our illumined awareness reveals itself as a greater amount of health, abundance, love and harmony. In the language of old this was stated as *things being added unto us.* Clearer language states it as *opening to greater awareness* of that which *is.* In incorporeal awareness, nothing needs to be (can be) "added"; nothing is missing.

Look into your room again and actively realize that even though everything you observe seems to be corporeal, *it is not.* Only incorporeality is. I observe incorporeal being as I observe you. I observe incorporeal form as I observe my couch, chairs, ottoman, table, the garden, the flowers, the trees, the colors, the sounds, the fragrances.

The entire universe and all it constitutes is the infinite variety of mind form. Mind does not observe form; mind *is* form. Your awareness is not aware *of* form, awareness *is* form. You are aware *as,* not aware *of.*

There is no such thing as unformed God or awareness — unmanifested, undemonstrated, invisible, intangible God or awareness. Awareness is not ethereal. The accepted notion of an ethereal vs. a palpable existence is, again, belief alone. We have differentiated what we believe is God or spirit (ethereal, incorporeal) from that which we believe is human,

physical and material (matter, corporeal). Such differentiation is untrue. God is one and omnipresent. Where can there
be differentiation in oneness, in omnipresence? Judge not
by the appearance. This does not only mean that we should
not judge physical appearance, it means that we should not
judge anything. Judge not by anything we can name or define; that we can see, hear, taste, touch, smell or imagine;
that we sense as being inner vs. outer; that we have learned.

For humanity, education is undeniably beneficial, of
course. In truth, it means nothing. We have to empty ourselves of every strand of our education in order to be available for the voice of God. "Neither do men put new wine
into old bottles: else the bottles break, and the wine runneth
out, and the bottles perish: but they put new wine into new
bottles, and both are preserved." (Matthew 9:17) "Be taught of
God." (John 6:45)

Only Awareness Itself is true. Once we are imbued with
Awareness Itself, we need no agency of knowledge or wisdom. We have lifted above and beyond all agency, including
the agency of education.

The Father, Awareness Itself, knows what you have need
of, and it is its good pleasure to give it to you. How? At every
point of the infinitude — the place whereon you stand —
there *is* the *fullness* of God, the utter and unconditional fulfillment of being within and without, visible and tangible as
Awareness Itself.

Fulfillment is unconditional. God *is,* and God is infinite
and omnipresent. Where, therefore, could there be condition, separateness, division? Or do we believe God sets conditions upon itself in order to experience the presence it
already is? The notion is ridiculous to entertain.

God *is,* therefore the God experience *is;* and *is,* of course,
already is. It's too late to be conditional. Fulfillment already
is because all *is* the presence of God, which is fulfillment.

All good, all knowledge, all wisdom, all direction is uncon-ditionally available to our immediate experience because all that God is is Awareness Itself — your awareness. Fulfill-ment is not produced or dispatched as we lift into Aware-ness Itself. All fulfillment exists right where you are this instant. Lifted awareness makes us *aware* of that which al-ready is, yet has until now been unseen. Good is not drawn to us as we pray, meditate, sit in class, and sit in silence, even though it may appear to be. Again, judge not by appearance. As you become ever more aware of *is,* you "draw all unto yourself" — your eyes are opened and you witness the fin-ished kingdom of fulfillment in all its visible glory right where you are, *as you.*

God Is

God *is;* the finished kingdom of Awareness Itself *is,* within and without.

"The heavens and the earth were finished, and all the host of them. And God blessed and sanctified [them]." (Genesis 2:1-3)

What more could we possibly want when seeking the clarity of truth? No matter what is believed about life. the world, and God, and how it is described, it isn't that. All is God itself which is unnameable, undefineable, indescrib-able. Heaven and earth (the objective sense) is God. The only existence is the *finished* existence of utter and uncon-ditional fulfillment.

The fact that we experience God three-dimensionally, objectively, in what seems to be an environment of cause and effect and time and space has no importance or conse-quence the minute we've lifted ourselves up into that which, in reality, all *is* — Awareness Itself or God consciousness. It has no consequence or validity because the only existence, the only presence, the only being, mind, body, thing, con-

dition, place, activity, and amount *is* God which cannot be
named or defined.

Names and definitions are good and useful only as long
as we do not believe that they are entities in themselves. Of
course we continue using them to operate and communicate
in the world. But it is only as we consciously know the truth
of everything we name and define, and let truth live and reveal *itself* as all in our awareness, that truth becomes available to our practical experience.

The truth is that only Awareness Itself is. Our family,
home, business, customers, clients, students; our markets,
produce and products, our world and all it contains are the
one presence of Awareness Itself sensed as an infinite variety
of different formations. Each form constitutes the whole,
and each *evidences* the whole as one with all.

Whatever the forms and activities of the moment consist
of — relationship, family, business, money, leisure — all is
the one substance, presence and form of Awareness Itself.
The *whole of fulfillment* exists as each form and activity.
Whatever we are aware of, *there is the whole of fulfillment already visible, tangible and practical, seen as and by that which it
is: Awareness Itself.*

In the Master's words, the Father [Awareness Itself]
knows what you have need of and it is his good pleasure to
give you the kingdom. The Father knows what you have
need of. Think — the Father, Awareness Itself, the whole
kingdom, already exists as the whole of you and everything
of your life. Everywhere you look there is nothing but the
whole of fulfillment — nothing of good is missing, nothing
is in lack or limitation, nothing is diluted, nothing is absent.
To material sense it appears as if there is much absence of
fulfillment. To material sense it appears as if God is absent
and nowhere to be found. It is the experience of millions of
people that the more they seek God the less he seems to be

available. It is true. Why? Because if we seek God as and for the human condition we seek amiss. "Ye ask, and receive not, because ye ask amiss." (James 4:3)

God is Awareness Itself; God is incorporeal. The corporeal *sense* we believe is real, isn't; it is not an entity. If that which we sense is unreal in and of its own self, we cannot evidence truth in, as or for it. Truth can only be evident, and is, as that which is real.

The good we believe we have need of already exists right where we believe it's needed — as visible, tangible, practical form. "The Father knows" means the Father *is*. The father *is* what you have need of, and it is its good pleasure to give it to you.

Our one actual need, no matter which of the thousands of guises the sense of need takes on, is to have our eyes opened to that which is. We need spiritual awareness, instead of human, material awareness. As soon as we truly live as and by spiritual awareness, we have instant freedom of sense and things. All that God is and has is ours. Earth as it is in heaven becomes real experience for us. It is called the healing consciousness.

A person who turns to our spiritual consciousness in need of healing finds him or herself healed quickly. Why? We know that the body is a body of Awareness Itself, not physical. We are not presented with a physical body to heal. We are living what the body actually is, and because Awareness Itself sees itself, the person's whole and healthy body is quickly evident in its presence existing as us.

The evidence — the image and likeness — is infallible as long as "we" are out of the picture allowing Awareness Itself to be all-of-all.

This is the light on the statement, Your Father knows what you have need of, and it is his good pleasure to give you the kingdom.

CHAPTER SIX

AWARENESS ITSELF
DOES THE WORK

Omniscience knows; and omniscience is Awareness Itself. Awareness Itself knows. Awareness Itself *is*.

Awareness Itself is the omnipresence of all good. No matter what presents itself to us — a person, thing or condition — it is the omnipresence of all good Aware of Itself.

Think about that statement. We could live with that for a year and awaken to more of its truth everyday. As a person, a thing, a condition presents itself to you, it is the omnipresence of all good, all that God is and has. It is not anything else because there isn't anything else it can be. Only God is. This is as clear to me as 4×4 is 16. Four x 4 cannot be less, cannot be more, and cannot be absent. Four × 4 *is* 16. We cannot separate 4×4 from 16 or 16 from 4×4. We do not have to be good to have 4×4 is 16. We do not have to apologize to all the people we've offended over the years. We do not have to repair our so-called karmic debt.

The only existence is that of *is,* God, Awareness Itself — which is unconditional and unconditionally present good. Four x 4 is 16 no matter what we do or fail to do throughout the rest of life. Likewise, God *is,* no matter what.

God is the only existence; God is *all* there is. All is Awareness Itself despite the way it *appears* to be through this or as this level of awareness. When we are looking through a stained-glass window, sunlight *appears* through the stained glass to be multicolored. Sunlight itself is never multicolored, but the stained-glass window makes it appear to be.

In the same way we observe, we experience, *through* this level of awareness. We call it "the mind," but it is our current level of awareness which makes the one presence appear to be objective, three-dimensional, here and there, the effect of a cause existing somewhere in space at a certain time. These, like the colored light, are all and only appearances of *the one* that never changes, that can never *be* changed because no other power exists to change it, can never be reduced or diluted because no other powers exist to reduce or dilute. If there were, whatever is changing, lessening or diluting God would have to be greater than omnipotence, which is nonsense.

No other exists and, certainly, no greater. God is the only; God is the almighty. God could not be the only and the almighty if there were something else and something mightier. Meditate deeply on this truth. Deep and consistent meditation is the key to realization.

Now that we have clear understanding that only Awareness Itself *is,* let us understand the miracle of good in our lives. We have heard that because only God is, only God *can.* In the language of this book, only Awareness Itself is; therefore only Awareness Itself *can.* How many times do we find ourselves needing to do something, achieve something, realize something: "If I can do this, I will have succeeded. If I can realize spirit sufficiently, I'll have sufficient spiritual realization to witness more good in my life. If I can know more about love, my relationship will be more beautiful, deeper, more meaningful, more joyous. If I can understand more about the life that God is, my body will be healthier and more youthful. I might be able to lose a little more weight and look better, or put a little more weight on and look better."

We believe that if we can set a good cause in motion, we will obtain our concept of a good effect. Belief is the root problem. Every belief has an opposite, and all belief is filled with desire. We can almost stand to the side of ourselves and watch belief in operation — especially spiritual belief: "If I can realize this truth or that truth I will be able to demonstrate it."

Now let's hear it again: Only Awareness Itself *is;* therefore only Awareness Itself *can.* You and I cannot because you and I are nothing in and of our own selves. If we believe we are something in and of our own selves, we get busy trying to "can" — I can or I might be able to or I will try to. I will give it my best effort. I will try to become more spiritual.

Haven't we been trying to become more spiritual since the day we first discovered God? We've been trying to attain spiritual realization since our first truth book or class. How many years ago is that for you? For me it was twenty — twenty years of trying to attain some measure of spiritual realization and miserably failing. Why do we miserably fail? *Because we of our own selves are nothing. Only God is; only Awareness Itself is.*

Let's think of the sun and the sunbeam. Can you imagine if the sunbeam believed itself to be separate from the sun? Of course it never can be, just as we can never be separate or separated from God, from truth, but *belief is experience; therefore belief-sense is experience.* If we're sensing falsely, if we're living as a personal sense of self, then that very believed existence will be our experience. Even though God is the only reality of us and our universe, it doesn't do us any good. If we believe or sense that we are separate, that we are different — and that therefore we ourselves have to succeed in life, including that we ourselves have to succeed in spiritual attainment because we're separate from God, we're different from God, we're human, not spiritual — then the discords and struggles of separation will be our experience.

Please friends, I urge you with everything I am, to hear this now. You have *never* been required to attain spiritual realization. Your very Awareness Itself *is* spiritual realization. You have never been required to do anything that will enable you to heal, to experience love, to experience prosperity, peace, harmony, joy, to be utterly fulfilled every hour of your life. You've never been required to do this yourself because there isn't a "your"-self. There is only God-self, individually here, right here as what the world calls "you."

Let's return to the sun and the sunbeam, assuming that the sunbeam believes she is different and separate, a personal sunbeam. Believing this, and therefore suffering much dark and cold, it makes sense that one day she will feel a stirring within and begin to study truth. As truth begins to alight within her, she will soon devote hours, years, and decades to attaining sun realization, trying to lift her awareness into the realization of oneness with the sun. *By making this effort she fails before she starts.* Do you see why?

She already *is* one with the sun; she is just *unaware* of it. The very belief that she is not, will block her from realized oneness, block her from experiencing the tangible presence of oneness. And it will block her *forever* until the day she wakes up and realizes *I am* one with the sun. *I am* the very presence of the sun.

If she studies as a believed separateness and difference from the sun, she will study for eternity and never "attain" her conscious oneness with the sun. The only way she will evidence conscious oneness with the sun is to wake up to the fact that her consciousness *is already* that of the sun because the sun *is* what she *is*. She would not exist if the sun did not, and the sun would not exist if the sunbeam did not. The sun and the sunbeam are one and the same existence. All that the sun is and has the sunbeam is and has because "one" and the "other" are the very same existence, form and activity. I live, yet not I, the sun lives my life. The sun is my Awareness Itself being individual and unique awareness as "me." And because the sun can never be unconscious of itself, my consciousness can never be unaware of its sun-ness.

The minute the sunbeam becomes aware of this one truth she experiences her freedom. She has awakened and her infinity and eternity are now conscious awareness instead of conscious unawareness.

In this way, *conscious awareness* of Awareness Itself is the greatest secret in all of heaven and earth.

You *are* the spiritual realization; you *are* the spiritual presence. You never have been separate. You never did have to study; you just had to wake up.

Once we know this, then we understand what all the classes and books are telling us — that we *are* the presence, but we have to *awaken* to this truth. Our eyes have to open. Nothing has to be achieved except awakening. Once we are awake to the truth of *is* — even by a grain — *is* quickly emerges through the fog we've lived with all this time, and harmony becomes evident. Harmony has been here all the time but we have been unable to see it through the fog.

Now when you reread any Miracle Self book and re-listen to any Miracle Self class with this awareness, watch how quickly you awaken. Watch how quickly all those classes and books come alive and fill your awareness with the living waters of realization. Every written and spoken word awakens you. You will not find one sentence that tells you you are absent of your oneness or absent of your good and that you have to find some way of attaining it, pleading with God to give it to you.

I am talking about true truth books, not metaphysics, but scientific truth books — books that speak of the one principle and practice of truth as taught and demonstrated by the Master Jesus the Christ and the great Prophets of the ages. There are not many such teachings; they are like the world's rarest diamond, so be careful.

True truth teachings — pure truth in which there is no mental, physical or material involvement ("Not by might, nor by power, but by my spirit, says the Lord of hosts"); where there is the understanding of both the nature of God and the nature of "this world" — are rare. The great majority of teachings that claim to be truth are not. The pure truth is available in the four Gospels and the rest of the New Testament; it is also found throughout the Old Testament but great spiritual discernment is needed. It is in The Gospel of Thomas and also in the Bhagavad Gita (in metaphoric form). Today you have it clearly and substantially throughout the Miracle Self and throughout Joel S. Goldsmith's Infinite Way (the widespread fruitage of these two teachings prove it). "By their fruits ye shall know them." Where there is impersonal self (healing, prosperity, love, harmony, peace, joy, fulfillment of purpose) there is God. Where there is a lack of these there is a lack of God consciousness.

The evident fruitage is the beginning, the continuation, and the end of knowing who is of God consciousness and who is not. "Narrow is the door, and difficult is the road which leads to life, and few are those who are found on it." (Matthew 7:14 Lamsa) If the fruits are lacking, truth is lacking. It's simple. If we see a vineyard barren of fruit, we're seeing a vineyard barren of its truth. It is not "in vineyard consciousness." If we want to learn how to plant a true vineyard, we go to the vineyard laden with fruit. Its fruit reveals its truth; and we know we can learn everything we need to about planting a true and abundant vineyard.

So when you look into the rare teachings of pure truth you will witness abundant fruitage. The teacher has the healing consciousness; he or she reveals God, where to material sense God is absent. Where there is spiritual fruitage, know you are safe. "Where the spirit of the Lord is, there is liberty."

Let's return to the sunbeam. Is the sunbeam of its own self capable of generating light and heat? Does it need to try? Of course not. The sunbeam, as it wakes up realizes that *only the sun is;* therefore only the sun *can.* If it believes that it needs to achieve something to fulfill its light and heat, it instantly switches its awareness to that which *is* the perfection of its existence, which is the sun itself. Once it has realized that it and the sun are the same existence, it rests and freely — and instantly — receives its fulfillment.

This truth of the sun and the sunbeam is the truth of God and man (humanity).

"The earth [the objective experience — everything from a single thought and a single breath, to everything that constitutes the universe] is the Lord's [the mind's, is that of Awareness Itself] and the fullness thereof" — not ours. Your breath is not yours; your thought, not even a single thought, is yours. Why? Because only God is.

We hear these truths, but we do not take them literally, nor do we live them throughout our experience and realize, Well if this is the truth (which it is) then, of course, even my breath isn't mine; my senses are not mine; my mind and body are not mine; my family, home, business, money and the things money buys are not mine.

He performs the thing that is appointed for me; and
many such things are with him. (Job 23:14)

Awareness Itself performs the thing that is appointed for
me. What is appointed for us? The very form of this moment is that which is appointed for us, and he performs it.
In other words, Awareness Itself is itself as itself objectively
sensed as and *for* us. Sense and the objects of sense have
nothing to do with the requirements, efforts and possession
of a personal self. Sense is not our responsibility or work;
rather it is the Father within me that does the works.

It does not matter how we may define what each moment
consists of. We might be meditating in the early hours of
the morning, sitting at our desk writing or working on a
project, giving a talk, gathering with family or friends,
preparing a meal or doing our housework. Whatever this
moment is sensed as consisting of, Awareness Itself is its entire substance, form and experience.

I am *the substance, form and experience of the moment. Therefore, the responsibility for the sensed forms of its fulfillment is Mine.*

I am fulfillment, *and* I am *visible and tangible as each moment's fulfillment.*

As long as I am *free in you to shine through your senses un-
clouded, you see and have the fulfillment of each moment freely sensed
as "this world's" fulfillment.*

When we know this truth and stop believing that a personal self called you or called me is living a separate and
different life from Awareness Itself, we stop taking responsibility for the nature, purpose and outcome of the moment.

It is not your or my responsibility to see and to have the
tangible forms of God, good. We cannot. We do not have a
faculty for seeing and for having truth. We are nothing of our
own selves. Only Awareness Itself is; therefore only Aware-

ness Itself is the visibility and tangibility of fulfillment.

What we have believed to be our personal selves is actually our body of awareness. We are divine being, spiritual being, incorporeal being, infinite being, omnipresent being, not finite, local, temporal, mental and physical human beings existing for only a short time in a material world. The seeming human existence and material universe have nothing to do with existence itself. Existence itself is Awareness Itself, and because Awareness is omnipresence, every form of awareness is and has all that Awareness Itself is and has.

Only Awareness Itself is able to present our true experience, just as only the sun itself is able to present the fully illumined and formed sunbeam. The sunbeam cannot do it. The sunbeam is not a separate self with its own faculties. Nothing in it can generate its own light and heat, its own visibility and fulfillment. Nor can we. We have believed we have personal lives and faculties, and we run on the fickle steam of that belief, but how quickly it fizzles and eventually, after a few decades at most, dies.

When we understand this we also understand the nature of every problem. The belief in a personal self is the only disease, the only poverty, the only injustice, the only birth and death. The moment the personal self is dropped and Awareness Itself is lived, problems no longer exist.

> He performs his covenant, and many such things are with him. (Job 23:14, Lamsa translation)

The word "covenant" is defined in Merriam-Webster as

> 1. a formal solemn agreement intended as binding
> 2. an undertaking or promise of legal validity such as a contract under seal; the document or writing containing the terms of the agreement or promise.
> 3. the promises of God as revealed in the scriptures, conditioned on certain terms on the part of humanity, such

as an agreement regarded as having been made between
God and Israel whereby Israel was to be faithful to God.

The spiritual meaning of "Israelites" is awakening ones,
those who are awakening to and following the light of truth.
"Faithful to God" means faithful as spiritual being, awakening to truth, faithful to Awareness Itself as being all, as God
itself as being all, rather than the belief in God *and* humanity, God *and* matter, God *and* thing and condition. In the
infinity of God there can be no *and.* Existence is one hundred percent God. God is God as God. Nothing else exists.
This is why the Master reminded us that "ye are gods". We
are spiritual being not human being. We are beings and
bodies of awareness not of mentality and physicality. As we
live as and by Awareness Itself, yielding everything of "our"
senses, Awareness Itself is, sees and has the forms of Itself
as us. Now we are aware spiritually not humanly, not materially, physically or mentally, and now everything we are
aware of is of Awareness Itself which is fulfillment.

Israel was to be faithful to God, and God was to protect
and bless his faithful people.

4. a promise regarded as having been enacted by God and
granting redemption and salvation to humanity [in other
words, redemption and salvation from belief] through . . .
[the consciousness of truth.]

Salvation comes as spiritual awareness, by the act of spir-
itualizing awareness, being aware of Awareness Itself being
all-of-all, and living by it.

When he, the spirit of truth, is come he will guide you
into all truth. (John 16:13)

"When he, the spirit of truth, is come . . ." means when

we lift or move into the awareness of Awareness Itself or when we leave humanity (materiality, physicality, mentality) behind, put it aside in the realization that it of its own self is nothing.

We do not have to do anything with belief because it is unreal. Hear it: We never have to do anything about that which *seems* to be. The very thing that seems to need our help, even urgent help, is a decoy. It does not need anything because what is actually present is the substance, form and visibility of God itself, where to material sense there seems to be bad or lack, limitation or disease.

What we need to do is lift *away* from the false sense of existence into truth where all *true* existence is visible and real. This is the only need. So, "When he the spirit of truth is come" means when we have lifted up into the awareness of Awareness Itself and are able to rest there and start *feeling* the presence in us and as us. That is when "he the spirit of truth is come" — is come into conscious awareness. We are now consciously aware of the presence of Awareness Itself, and as we rest in its felt presence, as we relax everything of us, as we let go, we fall back empty, a nothingness, a vacuum. It is at this point that our eyes are opened and we see as Awareness Itself is as and "through" us.

Remember, *he* performs; we do not. Our previously closed eyes are opened. We experience our ever-existent spiritual awareness objectively sensed as the good forms of our lives as we rest in the *feeling* of the presence of God. The consciously experienced presence of God opens our eyes to what we and all truly are. He performs — we do not; we rest and witness.

Right here we have the whole key to spiritual living: We rest in the felt presence and we witness. That's it. We're not involved; we're not assistants to God, and we cannot be. We rest in the presence and we witness, just like the sunbeam.

She rests and witnesses. She is not a personal sunbeam having to make effort for her own light and heat, struggling to meet the demands of the day. She rests and witnesses the infinity of the sun being all she is, has, and experiences.

> . . . he will guide you into all truth. (John 16:13)

There it is again: *he* will guide you. Awareness Itself will guide you.

The guiding and revealing presence is explained like this:

> The Comforter, which is the Holy Spirit, whom the Father will send in my name, he shall teach you all things, and bring all things to your remembrance, whatsoever I have said unto you.
> (John 14:26)

The comforter is the Holy Spirit. The comforter, the spirit, is Awareness Itself, the "he [that] shall teach you all things". It is the felt presence of Awareness Itself that teaches us, that opens our eyes to the truth of *all* things. This is why the Holy Spirit is called the comforter by the Master. Indeed, spirit is very comforting because with it we have truth made evident throughout our experience. The truth that is made evident throughout our experience is Awareness Itself being experienced as itself.

We must know this truth and then be satisfied with the experience of Awareness Itself *as* itself. Why "as itself"? Because all formation is the body of Awareness Itself, sensed objectively as the multitude of forms that constitute our universe. The one form is sensed as multitudinous form through mind that is, at our current level of awareness, objective, three-dimensional, infinite in variety. We witness so-called bodies of awareness, but each body (form, thing) is not a container of finiteness. Each form is the infinity and omnipresence of awareness. You are that; I am that; all is that.

The Father (I) will send the comforter, the Master assured the disciples. When you reach up into Me, not a person but into truth, then that truth will send, will *be,* the instant comforter. The moment we touch the hem of Awareness Itself, the very moment we even begin to feel the presence of Awareness Itself, we have the comforter, and because the comforter is never and cannot be unformed, invisible, intangible, we instantaneously have the form of the comforter — the good, the healing, the sufficiency, the food, the life, the love.

However, all form is, despite the way it is sensed, always and only ever Awareness Itself. Never seek Awareness Itself looking like a physical body, you'll fail; looking like material dollars, you'll fail; looking like human love, you will fail. Be satisfied with Awareness Itself as Itself as all-of-all. Then your senses are (and remain) clear. Belief is not clogging them. They are free to witness the image and likeness of Awareness Itself.

The mind is the faculty of awareness. Kept free of belief, our senses are unclogged and free to witness the image and likeness of Awareness Itself being all form, and all is good.

> I will put my spirit in you, and ye shall live. . . . (Ezekiel 37:14)

"I [Awareness Itself] will put my spirit in you . . ." I will fill your awareness with Me, with Awareness Itself. Can you hear the sunbeam realizing this, reading its book of truth? I, the sun, will put my spirit (my light and heat) in you ". . . and you shall live". *I will put my spirit in you, and you will live.*

Good is automatic and infallible as we realize that Awareness Itself is *all,* as we reach up into Awareness Itself, seek nothing but Awareness Itself, rest in Awareness Itself, open to the experience of Awareness Itself being itself as all, and being satisfied with the experience. In this way, we have the keys to the kingdom of good, the very kingdom of God; and our lives are infallibly and automatically fulfilled. We are filled with life itself.

Some may call it miraculous healing; others may call it the multiplication of loaves and fishes or dollars or business success or opportunity opening its doors; still others may call it homes for the homeless, clothes for the naked, safety for those who are under threat, security for the insecure, love where there seems to be an absence of love. As the Master stated it, I am come that you may have life and have it more abundantly. *I am come into conscious awareness.*

> . . . I will pour out of my spirit upon all flesh . . . (Acts 2:17)

"Flesh" means objective sense, form: I will fill objective sense to overflowing with me, with the truth, with visibility and clarity, with *truthful* objective sense.

There is nothing wrong with objective sense in itself. If there were something wrong with flesh, spirit couldn't pour itself into it. Oh no, there is nothing wrong with flesh; flesh is the spiritual presence and form simply *sensed objectively* as what we name and define as person, thing and condition. We sense the one body of Awareness conceptually. The concept of flesh — that which we call the human body and the material thing — is unreal in and of itself; it is simply a body of awareness in our experience.

I will pour out of *My* spirit, of *Myself* — *Awareness Itself will pour itself upon all flesh, upon all objective sense.*

> Know you not that you are the temple of God, and that the Spirit of God dwells in you? (1 Corinthians 3:16)

"Do you not know [are you unaware] that you are the temple of God [you are the body of Awareness Itself] and that the Spirit of God [the visibility and reality of Awareness Itself] dwells in you?" It always has, but we have believed and entertained a prodigal sense.

A teacher once said, "There is a church service going on inside of you twenty-four hours a day, but are *you there?*" Do you not know that you are *the* temple of God, the very formation, the very being, the very awareness, the very body, the very universe of God, of Awareness Itself, and that the spirit, the alive awareness, the visible presence of God, of Awareness Itself, dwells in you, is what you are, is the very substance, form and flesh of you?

> For it is God which works in you both to will and to do
> of his good pleasure. (Philippians 2:13)

It is both the presence of, the eternal unchanging existence of (as the will of God), and the activity of God itself that do his good pleasure, that awaken us, that open our eyes to truth. The Master explained it like this:

> Fear not, little flock; for it is your Father's good pleasure
> to give you the kingdom. (Luke 12:32)

> For it is not you that speak, but the Spirit of your Father
> which speaks in you. (Matthew 10:20)

When we hear the word "speak(s)," realize that it means both the truth and the form — the Word as the form of itself as you. When you think, when you act, it is not you that speaks but "the Spirit of your Father which speaks in you". It is Awareness Itself being individual you, as your immediately apprehensible truth of sense.

If we take ownership of our being and the things that constitute our experience, we lock the kingdom of God out of sense. If we believe our mind is ours, our body is ours, our money is ours, our business is ours, our family is ours, we personalize and finitize our experience of them by that belief. This belief in me-my-mine, in personal self, has cut out the *entire* infinity and omnipresence of all truthful experience from our sense.

We have taken over what is not ours; we have "hijacked God" and now we have to suffer it. But hear this: "It is not you that speaks. . . ." It is not you that lives, not you that does anything (or is even capable) ". . . but the Spirit of your Father which speaks in you". It is the presence of Awareness Itself that speaks in you, which sees, hears, tastes, touches, smells, acts, thinks in and as you.

"The earth [the whole objective sense] is the Lord's [the mind's, awareness's] and the fullness thereof." So give it to Awareness; give it to the Lord; give it to God. Surrender the self and yield to the presence of God right here in practical experience.

> The Spirit itself bears witness with our spirit, that we are the children of God. (Romans 8:16)

It is the "Spirit itself that bears witness with our spirit" because I and the Father are one. The Father is *I; I* is the Father. As we know this truth and yield our *sense* of *I* to *I itself* we have made ourselves empty and available for *I itself* to bear witness as our I.

Only God is; therefore only God can. Only God Itself — Awareness Itself, Spirit Itself — sees itself as it is. We have heard these truths throughout the Miracle Self teachings, and here Romans 8 gives it to us "officially." The particular words used for a statement of truth today are no less authoritative than those used two thousand years ago, as long as they do not come from a personal sense or intellect, but are the voice of God itself coming through a transparency of self. The teachings of the Miracle Self (and the Infinite Way) are the voice of God coming to us through the window or transparency of teacher. They are modern-day scripture.

"It is the Spirit that bears witness" because only spirit can see itself; we cannot. Only Awareness Itself can see itself as individual being *and does,* if we will let it. "I live; yet not I, but Christ lives in me." (Galatians 2:20) Use any true synonym you prefer for the word "Christ" — Awareness Itself lives me, God itself lives me, spirit itself lives me, consciousness itself lives me, infinity itself lives me.

I live, yet not I, infinity itself lives me. Isn't that a wonderful truth to wake up to each morning? Infinity lives me as all that I am, have, see and experience.

I live; yet not I, omnipresence lives me. I live; yet not I, love lives me as all that I experience universally. I live yet not I, life itself lives me as all of my universal experience. *If we yield* and let it, *then* we witness it; *then* we have it as real and practical experience.

> For the Holy Spirit shall teach you in the same hour what you ought to say. (Luke 12:12)

Do not take this statement as literally as it sounds. Existence is not divided into different departments — presence vs. speech vs. sight vs. hearing vs. touch. All is one, and all is present and active as one. The *whole* is the only, and that whole is indivisible, inseparable.

Knowing this, we can read this and any scripture with greater spiritual discernment. "For the Holy Spirit [Awareness Itself] shall teach you [shall reveal to you] in the same hour [in this moment of now] what you ought to say." It reveals to you what you hear coming out of your mouth, the truth of form, the truth of being, the truth of awareness, the truth of love, relationship, money, business.

The Holy Spirit shall teach you, shall reveal to you. *He performs,* not we ourselves. Awareness Itself performs. Father-Mother existence performs, not we ourselves. "For it is not ye that speak, but the Spirit of your Father which speaketh in you." (Matthew 10:20)

> ... Not by might, nor by power, but by my spirit, says the Lord of hosts. (Zechariah 4:6)

"Says the Lord of hosts" means, says the unconditioned mind — the Lord (mind) of hosts (form); says the truth of experience, existence, being, form, body, thing, amount, place, condition. "Not by might [not by physical effort], nor by power [not by mental effort or manipulation], but by my spirit."

In other words, here we are faced with what is, according to sense testimony, a human problem of disease or lack or limitation or poverty or homelessness; a tsunami, tornado, earthquake, contagion, or war. We are faced with what *seems* to be a very real and pressing physical or material problem and, according to appearance, what seems to need a mental or physical solution.

But the voice of truth says: "Not by might" — not by physical or material effort or reliance — "nor by power" — nor by mental effort, persuasion, or manipulation, including not by the effort to become spiritual enough so that God will solve the named and defined problem for us.

Remove all might and all power from yourself and what do you have left? You are a heap of personal self nothingness, along with me, and the Master himself. "I can do nothing of my own self: as I hear, I judge: and my judgment is just [my awareness is true]; because I seek not my own will, but the will of the Father which has sent me." (John 5:30)

In other words, I can do nothing by my own effort, but I can witness everything being done "by my spirit, says the Lord of hosts." The Lord of Hosts means the truth of form, the truth of the objective sense or earth. The Lord of hosts is telling us not to use human, material or physical effort, to drop all effort to heal the problem. The problem does not exist in God; it is merely belief. Leave it alone, and turn to Awareness Itself.

Why on earth would the prophet be telling us to do nothing of our own selves when the problem facing us obviously requires its opposite as the solution? Because there are no opposites in God. Where the problem seems to be, nothing except God actually is. And because God is eternal, unchanging existence, the form which to sense testimony appears diseased or discordant is actually healthy and harmonious this instant.

The prophet knows that the problem is nothing but a false sense of the one presence, which is Awareness Itself. Ignore the false sense and get up into Awareness Itself. There you will discover that as you sit resting, feeling the presence, and as you are satisfied with that experience, Awareness Itself pours through the senses and reveals itself as the only truth of being, mind, body, thing, condition, and amount.

> It is the spirit that quickens; the flesh profits nothing: the words that I speak unto you, they are spirit, and they are life. (John 6:63)

"It is the spirit that quickens . . ." Quickens what? Quickens our senses, quickens our awareness, opens our eyes more quickly to that which *is*. ". . . the flesh [the objective sense of and effort toward being, body and world] profits nothing." There we go again: Only God is; therefore only God can. We are nothing of our own selves; therefore we cannot do anything *for* our own selves. We *believe* we can; we believe we can manipulate the body and the material world, but, honestly, how long does any manipulation (even if we do succeed) last? It doesn't last long, does it? Nothing of material or physical good in itself lasts. Why? Because it is only belief; it does not have any law or substance, principal, presence, form, visibility to sustain itself in experience. It is merely imagery.

If we succeed in manipulating imagery, because it of itself has no substance, form, law, or principle to it, it soon fades away or disintegrates, and we're left at square one, usually worse than we were to begin with. We now need even more health, even more money, even more love. The good things and conditions of belief disintegrate in front of us just as we believe we can start relying on them. We cannot rely on them: ". . . the flesh profits nothing." The form, the image, profits nothing; that which we sense in and of its own self profits nothing. It is the *spirit* that quickens, the *spirit* that reveals the *truth* of form.

". . . [T]he words that I speak unto you, they are spirit and they are life." In other words, the truth you are hearing or feeling is spirit, is Awareness Itself, is God itself welling up within and becoming known. The experience of truth welling up within is Awareness Itself, and so of course you now become aware.

The *I* of you has no personal self in it whatsoever. *I* is the very presence of God in you and as you, so the words *I* speak to you, they are spirit and they are life, they are the very form, substance, visibility of all good, the truthful image and likeness, the finished kingdom of fulfillment, earth as it is in heaven. The very word *I* speak *is* the form of itself objectively sensed by you and by me.

Now do you see why the Master instantaneously healed the multitudes? The very word *I* speak, the very spirit *I am is itself* the form objectively witnessed. No such thing as unformed, unmanifested, undemonstrated, invisible, intangible, impractical God exists. The Master is telling us this: the very presence of me and the very words *I* speak to you are not mine myself but are the Father's who sent me, so they themselves *are* the visible, tangible presence of your true mind, your true body, your true family, your true money, your true business, your true world conceptually sensed.

When you read or hear statements of scripture, realize that the *very word itself is* the visible form revealed. Watch how quickly the visible form of good is visible to *your sense* as you know this truth, rest in it, and trust it.

These words are not information *about* truth. They are the *very word itself,* the very presence of the visible, tangible truth itself. "The words that I speak unto you, they are spirit, and they are life."

CHAPTER SEVEN

THE INFINITY
OF ALL THINGS

I is the light that *is* God. *I* is Awareness Itself which is all and constitutes all-of-all that God is, that good is, that fulfillment is — all. No matter how we describe all, whether we describe it as ethereal or palpable, inner or outer, *I* (or Awareness Itself) *is* and constitutes the all-of-all that truth, that God is; all that visible, tangible truth is.

"The words that I speak unto you, they are spirit, and they are life." (John 6:63) The presence of God on earth does not *produce* healing, *produce* peace and harmony, *produce* fulfillment but *is itself* these. The very words I share with you — the words you are aware of on this page — are the spirit (substance) and the life (form), visibly so, real, practical, right here where you are, and where I am.

Being aware of Awareness Itself, seeking nothing but Awareness Itself for itself is the key, *is itself* the spirit and the life, visibly so, tangibly so. Awareness and form are one. The fact that you are aware of these words as spirit and as life is the visible, tangible substance and form of them in your immediate experience. But again, you must know this truth and then rest in it, to experience it.

Look at the far side of your room, the wall, a painting, the window, a flower. Now your awareness is filled with objective sense. Your faculties are busy, processing that which you believe is real, that which you have affixed your awareness to. Now pull your awareness back into the middle space between you and the object you observe. Become aware of Awareness Itself. Now rather than believing that you are aware *with* your awareness, *of* an object, begin to realize that Awareness Itself is all "three": *you,* the awareness you are aware *with,* and the *object* of awareness. Feel Awareness Itself "happening" as or within you.

(A few minutes of silence)

You cannot really define the seemingly empty space you are now aware of. Nothing exists there to name, define, attach to. Because you have now moved your awareness into the nameless undefinable, you are instantly free of name and definition, of good and bad, of physical limitations and laws. You exist in the world but not of it. You are the unencumbered self — free in Awareness Itself, devoid of burden, of need, of desire, of problem, even free of human good, which is at best finite, temporal good, the good end of good-and-bad. You are free in the realm of truth. As you remain there you will quickly see it as objective good in your body and world.

You are now aware as infinity, as omnipresence, without being contained, without limitation — without beginning or end, birth or death, here or there, shape, size, amount, place, condition, good vs. bad.

You are aware as Awareness Itself when you are unable to define your awareness — when you are empty of self and objectivity, bathing in the middle space. You are aware of Awareness Itself; you *feel* the substance, the presence, the warmth, the love.

This is the entire key. As you feel the presence of Awareness Itself and as you relax in it and *as* it, as you let go of everything you can describe yourself as being, everything you sense you may need or want, and truly begin to *let Awareness Itself live as itself for itself as you and your world,* you are being the spirit and the life which is quickly evident as objective fulfillment.

Truth is now tangible in you, "closer than breathing, nearer than hands and feet". You are the spirit (the substance) and the life (the form) that is objectively sensed as good (God) people, things and conditions.

No Inner vs. Outer

There is no inner vs. outer in Awareness Itself or in our sense of awareness. As long as we do not attach awareness to person or thing, our awareness is omnipresence. You can demonstrate this in seconds.

Bring your awareness again to the center of your room, detached from all objects. Rest there for a few seconds. Is there an inner or an outer to your awareness?

There is none.

Is there an area of your awareness that is less full of awareness than another area?

There is none.

Awareness is omnipresence.

Bring your awareness to the nearest object in your room; now to the center of your room; and now through the window to the farthest place you can see. Isn't it true that your Awareness Itself is as full and alive "right here" as it is "all the way over there"?

Awareness has no inner or outer. Awareness is omnipresence. The infinitude is Awareness Itself, God itself. And because awareness can only see itself, what we are aware of as our universe is a vast array of awareness-forms. Because all is Awareness Itself, all form is visible, tangible infinity and omnipresence.

There is no separation or difference in Awareness Itself. There is no invisible vs. visible, intangible vs. tangible. There is no different place or state. There is no different experience. There is only one, which is Awareness Itself and the body of Awareness Itself, which is the visible, tangible form, no matter where you are aware (or of what or whom).

Wherever you are, there *I am.* Wherever you place your awareness, your thought, your sense, there *I am.*

Living the Rested State of Being

As you learn to live in and as the finished kingdom of Awareness Itself you live a rested state of being. You do not mentalize or labor for good; you rest, behold, and serve. You live twenty-four hours a day as the rested self — the peaceful, spacious, open, receptive-to-spirit, receptive-to-Awareness Itself — self. "I live yet not I, Christ lives my life" (or Buddha or Awareness Itself, God, spirit lives my life).

I live a deeper realm of awareness than sense testimony alone. I live Awareness Itself which is beyond or deeper than objective sense. The *I* that *I am* is Awareness Itself which constitutes all that God is and has; all that *is* God.

Remember that our objective sense does not change or dilute the presence of God. The forms that we witness *are* the fullness of God. When we know this truth, and when we seek nothing but that pure Awareness Itself instead of things and qualities of the world, "the Father's good pleasure" enables our sense to detect the presence of fulfillment instead of the appearing discord, lack and limitation of belief.

But we have to know the truth in order to be set free in truth. Without knowing the truth, we cannot see truth. Our senses are blocked because of the belief in two-ness, in separation, in difference.

Now let us get back into the middle space, the space in between — the seeming nothingness, the thin air devoid of objectivity. Realize that what seems to be empty space is in fact the fullness of Awareness. Feel the presence and activity of awareness within. Feel the unencumbered self, feel the freedom, feel the limitlessness of Awareness Itself. You may feel it as warmth, as peace, as a sense of release, a sense of joy or bliss, a sense of being in the arms of God, safe and protected.

Now move your awareness into the center, the substance, of an object. Realize that the object, although appearing to be solid, structural, of a particular size, shape and location, is actually a body of awareness. Rest your awareness in its body of awareness. Realize that "all three" — you, the object, and the awareness you are aware with, is the *one* presence and activity of Awareness Itself.

(Rest, feeling, being aware of Awareness Itself for a moment)

Rest in the presence more deeply, relaxedly, confidently. Deeply let go, and simply behold the experience of Awareness Itself existing as you and your environment.

Even though you are aware of the object, remain as Awareness Itself so that the object is entirely un-interesting to you, in itself. It is just an *is* in your experience; therefore it cannot have any good or bad quality about it, in itself. It

cannot tempt you to want something for it or from it, in itself, because you know that it is actually a body of Awareness
and is therefore the fullness of God itself.

As we feel (as we are aware of) the presence living within,
we *have* the infinity and omnipresence of fulfillment. Experiencing (feeling) the presence *is* the experience of fulfillment. It is done. Then, within a few minutes, hours, or days
we see the objective sense of it as what the *world* calls material fulfillment.

The feeling, the experience, is the spirit and the life.
"The words I speak unto you are spirit [are the substance,
the presence] and the life [the form, the visibility, the tangible, palpable, practical, reality right here where you are
and throughout your consciousness]" — the true image and
likeness; the fullness of good.

It is true that there is no absence of God anywhere
throughout infinity but because God is Awareness, it takes
our conscious *awareness* of the presence of God — feeling
the presence, experiencing the presence within — in order
to see it as so-called outer presence. Our senses must be
clear of materiality to be clear for God experience.

As we feel the presence of Awareness Itself (even in or as
body, person, thing, condition), we are being that which all
truthfully is. We are being a god which is the one state of
being that evidences God.

The key is being aware of Awareness Itself, not attaching
to or becoming entwined in that which seems to be, not attempting to demonstrate transformation in the outer, but
rather, knowing that no transformation is necessary. All already *is*. Anything that seems to need change is a lie, a false
picture. God stands right where the false picture suggests
an absence of God. And because God is fully visible and tangible as itself to itself for itself, the minute we are being
what God is (Awareness Itself) the objective sense of God

becomes evident to us as the fulfillment of person, thing and condition. We must *be* a god in order to see God-like form. To see and to have life, abundance, love and harmony, we must be that which they truly are — and that is Awareness Itself. We must be the presence of Awareness Itself. Then we are being the truth of form, the truth of being, the truth of body, the truth of amount, condition, place, universe. It is when we are being it that we see it; we can only see what we are being.

Where the Spirit of the Lord Is, There Is Liberty

The word "Lord" in scripture means mind. Where the light of mind is, where the spirit of the Lord is, there is liberty. In other words, we have to *be* the *spirit* of all in order to see the spirit (truth) of form. We cannot *be* spirit within and matter without. We have to be Awareness Itself as all.

See the entirety of your world as your children, or as the Master described it, his sheep, his flock. You are the god of your universe. "Ye are gods" (Psalm 82:6; John 10:34) What will we not do for our children? We want each and every one of our children, each and every person, thing and place in our world, to be free in truth, to be full of life, full of harmony, love, joy, purpose fulfilled. There is only one way of it. Hear the Master again: "I am the light of the world". I am the life, the love, the home, the food, the happiness and fulfillment of the world (the objective sense). *I* am. And what is *I?* Awareness Itself.

I am the light. *I* am that which illumines, which makes truth visible in tangible experience. *I* is Awareness Itself. We have to be the Awareness Itself unto our world so that the forms of Awareness Itself are revealed truthfully, which is as all that God is and has.

As we are *being* Awareness Itself in form — as we observe people, as we observe body, as we observe amount, as we observe our businesses, our practices, our teachings, as we observe our relationships, as we *are* our relationships, as we *are* family, as we are being our world as the presence of Awareness Itself — we are *being that presence* which reveals the truth of all.

Always remember — only Awareness Itself sees itself. Isn't that enough to realize?

We have to be the very presence of Awareness Itself radiating as the entirety of our consciousness, the entirety of our universe, the entirety of every moment-by-moment experience, *for* these. We have to be the substance of these *for* these. No one can do this for us, even God itself. Everything that can be done, God has already done by being all of all. It is now up to us, each and every one individually, to be what God is by yielding to God and letting God be and see and do for us.

We *are* individual God being, omnipresent God being, infinite God being. We are each the only presence of God on earth as far as our individual demonstration goes. There is no God out there able to demonstrate for us. God is already demonstrated. We have to awaken and be that which is already demonstrated. We have to be Awareness Itself in order to have the awareness — the visibility — of God as it is on earth.

We do not have to *do* anything with Awareness Itself because Awareness Itself is already the finished kingdom which constitutes all that God is and has, inside you and outside you. All that God *is* is already done, whether we call it ethereal or palpable, spiritual or material, divine or human. These are our misguided definitions of the one God, the one existence that we are, the one omnipresent God, the one omnipresent good.

The word *one* alone should root out of us all belief in separateness, difference, division. Only oneness is. The whole of oneness exists at every point of the infinitude at the same time, and is made real and visible to our sense as we abide as Awareness Itself and feel Awareness Itself abiding in us. We are not required to mentalize or convert Awareness Itself into our tangible fulfillment. Awareness Itself already *is* within and without.

The only state of being that believes the outer is separate and different from the inner is the personal self. But "I of my own self am nothing". If the personal self is nothing of its own self, everything it believes is also nothing. If we have not yet awakened to this, and continue attempting to demonstrate what the personal sense of self believes it needs, we are being fooled by belief, the devil.

"Get thee hence Satan." Ignore belief and realize *I am. I already am;* and because *I am, I have.* I do not need to become, to achieve, to attain. *I am,* and *I am all. I* am all-of-all within and without, the one presence, visible, tangible, real, here, now.

We only have to *be* Awareness Itself to see its earth forms clearly and fully. We have to be the one presence of truth — alive, alight, visible, real, practical. And what is that truth? Awareness Itself. Awareness Itself never has become something else, something separate, something different. The inner is the outer and the outer is the inner. Why then would we have to convert Awareness Itself to something different in the outer? Why would we need fulfillment in what we believe is a different state of form or being or body or awareness in order to tangibly have it? No different state of anything exists, no different state of awareness. Only Awareness Itself exists.

As you live as Awareness Itself, knowing the great secret that Awareness Itself *is all,* that Awareness Itself is the finished kingdom of heaven and earth and all the host of them, and continuously yield your sense of awareness to Awareness Itself, then Awareness Itself lives your life.

Awareness Itself exists inside you and outside you, there being no difference between inner and outer. As you live, yet not you, Awareness Itself lives your life; as you see, but do not see, Awareness Itself sees itself as you and for you; as you hear, but do not hear, Awareness Itself hears itself as you and for you; as you taste but do not taste, Awareness Itself tastes itself as you and for you; as you touch, but do not touch, Awareness Itself touches itself as you and for you; as you smell but do not smell, Awareness Itself smells itself as you and for you; as you think, but do not think, Awareness Itself thinks as itself as you and for you; as you act, but do not act, Awareness Itself acts as itself for you and as you.

In this way (and only in this way) is truth visible and tangible throughout your experience. Then (and only then) do we have life and nothing but life, with nothing that can touch that life. If Awareness Itself is living Itself as the only existence as us, through us, for us, what can touch our life? What can affect, what can damage, our life? What can be sick, injured or diseased? What negative, destructive powers can cause these mis-experiences? None exist. Only oneness exists.

As Awareness Itself lives itself as us, for us, through us, where is limit? Where is lack? Where is an absence of good, when good and abundance are Awareness Itself, which has no limit, which *is* the infinite itself, which *is* omnipresence itself; which, as we experience it, *is the spirit and the life*. The words I speak unto you, the presence happening in you, as you, *are* the spirit and the life.

Nothing else exists. Nothing else has to happen. Awareness Itself is all, visible, real, right here where you are — the *I* that *is* the spirit and life of all. Human sense describes the forms of *I* as material abundance, dollars, opportunity, doors opening, success, but we know nothing of the sort is true.

We know that Awareness Itself is all of all, and is already and forever whole and complete. As we are *being* Awareness Itself unto our world, never slipping out of Awareness Itself, we are the light of the world; we are the light of truthful world; we are the illumined, truthful, visible evidence, the visible illumined form, the reality of our experience.

Do you catch that you have to *be* that which God is for all in your world? If you are not being the god of your world, the people, things and conditions of your world cannot reveal their truth to you. Truth cannot reveal itself to any individual who is not being what truth is. Just as the sunbeam has to be what the sun is in order to reveal light and the heat throughout its universe, so we must be a god in order to evidence God as our world. We have to *be* the suns of and for our world. We have to be the spirit and the truth. Do you see? We are the gods of our universe, so we have to *be* that god. And what is that exactly? Precisely how do we evidence truth where there seems to be none (or very little), or seems to be a problem that will not yield? How precisely do we *be* the god, the light of our world? *Being aware of Awareness Itself is the key.*

Being the very being of Awareness Itself, empty of personal self, *letting and beholding* the radiance of Awareness *being* the forms of itself throughout our world — this is the way.

Boundless Supply

Because Awareness is boundless and omnipresent, supply and its forms, including dollars, are boundless and omnipresent.

Take a dollar in your hand. To material sense the dollar seems to be a limited, material form. It is worth only what the number printed on it states. If that number is *one* we cannot even buy a cup of coffee with it today. No matter what the number states — one hundred, one thousand, one hundred thousand, one million — our money is worth only that amount and not more. All amount is limited amount to material sense.

Let us assume that the amount we have available is too little to meet the financial demands being made upon us this week or this month. What are we to do? Do we actually have only the limited amount of money material sense suggests we have? What did the Master do when it appeared as if he and the disciples had only five loaves and two fishes between them, yet five thousand hungry men plus women and children too faced him?

"I am the light of the world." I am the light of the food; I am the light of the dollar that reveals a boundless and omnipresent amount of form right where the need seems to be. What is that light? Awareness Itself, unencumbered Awareness Itself — awareness with no *thing* in it, no person in it, no condition in it — just Awareness Itself, pure, limitless, omnipresent Awareness Itself. This is the light of the world. This is the light of the food that witnesses all the food unto the sufficiency of the hour or the sense of need. This is the light of the dollar that witnesses all the dollars necessary unto this hour, unto this circumstance, unto this place, unto this sense of need. There is no actual need, there is no actual place, there is no actual circumstance or condition that needs anything apart from the *one* need that is the immediate fulfillment of person, thing and condition, and that *one* is Awareness Itself.

"Feed my sheep." (John 21:16-17) Feed your dollars, your business, your products and services, your customers. Bring dollars to mind for a moment, knowing that they are truly forms of awareness, then drop them. You need not consider them again. Why? Because Awareness Itself is what they truly are. We never need take thought for the form in itself. Our awareness of Awareness Itself takes care of its image and likeness in our experience.

All form is God form (because only God exists); all form is real. But if we do not know what form is, believing it to be what its material appearance suggests, form can only be to us what belief says it is. Then we are stranded in material sense with form that appears to be separate and different from infinity. *If we are aware of a thing, it is the form of Awareness Itself because Awareness Itself is all that we are aware of.* Know dollars as forms of awareness; forget about the material appearance of the dollar and bring your awareness to Awareness Itself. Know that there is no such thing as limited form. Form is as limitless and omnipresent as Awareness Itself because all *is* Awareness Itself.

Now lift into Awareness Itself. "He looked up to heaven" (Matthew 14:19) — he raised his awareness into the incorporeal, the heavenly presence, Awareness Itself. Feel Awareness Itself. Fall in love with Awareness Itself — "love God with all your heart, all your soul, all your mind, and all your strength." Feel and immerse yourself and become saturated with the experience of Awareness Itself flowing within you.

Whether it takes you a second or ten seconds or ten minutes or all day long, it doesn't matter. Get to that place where you begin to feel Awareness Itself — where you feel the unencumbered true you, where all belief in matter and amount, where all burdens have dropped from your shoulders, where you feel the presence of God, feel the presence of Awareness Itself flowing freely within.

This very experience is the light unto money, is the light unto food, home, relationship, harmony in the world. This very experience is the revealing truth, the revealing truth of every form including the form we call money. This very experience is itself the tangible and visible infinity of form, the ever-present fulfillment of the scenery, of the moment, of the seeming need.

Never attempt to spiritually multiply dollars, business or success. You will fail. When we *be* Awareness Itself unto the form that appears to be dollars, Awareness Itself reveals its image and likeness "through us" as the fulfillment of the sensed scenery or need. Fulfillment *is,* and becomes seen as we *be* that which it is. Its presence as us is witnessed as the perfect sufficiency of dollars unto the need, unto the circumstance, unto the claim. Then, one way or another, we behold the multiplication of dollars fulfilling the need — the multiplication of opportunity, customers, food, home, safety, security, health, love — usually with twelve baskets full left over.

How it appears through objective sense matters not. It is automatically and infallibly witnessed because we are being the very presence of the truth of dollars, of the condition fulfilled, of the place fulfilled, of the hunger fulfilled, of the peace fulfilled, the harmony fulfilled, the perfection revealed.

Do you see?

It is like being the magnet of good on earth. When we are being the presence of Awareness Itself, we are like the world's mightiest magnet drawing to itself all the good of earth whether (in appearance) that good is dollars, food, healthy flesh, love, friendship, companionship, home, clothes, opportunity, or business success.

It doesn't matter how we describe the miracle of form. It isn't that. It is the very presence of truth, the unconditional and ever-present truth now being made visible to us, not because it suddenly arrived from God's storehouse in the sky by our prayers of petition, but because our eyes are now open to that which is, instead of closed, seeing that which isn't.

Realize that as the awareness of Awareness Itself is maintained, we are, this instant, the magnet of the world, the spirit and life of the world that draws to it all the good of the world and limitlessly so.

CHAPTER EIGHT

AN ACT OF AWARENESS

The key to experiencing Awareness Itself living your life is to maintain your sense of awareness on and yielded to Awareness Itself. Keep your mind filled with Awareness Itself, aware of, yet unattached to, the objective forms (people, things and conditions) of the world. Be in the world but not *of* it. Be of Awareness Itself.

You do not cease from living and operating in the world; you do not leave your family, your friends, your business; you do not stop eating, using money, wearing clothes and having your hair cut; you do not move to a cave and live a hermit's life. Your existence as Awareness Itself in the world fulfills your purpose: to be the light of the world in your individual and unique way.

Existence and all it constitutes is Awareness Itself. Nothing that exists is separate, different or less than the fullness of Awareness Itself. "All things were made by him; and without him was not anything made that was made." (John 1:3) Because all is Awareness Itself, the key to evidencing the truth of all lies in our use of awareness. As we use awareness as it *is* (within and without) it reveals its true image and likeness throughout our lives. If we use awareness as it is not (humanly, materially) all we witness is degrees of belief.

Using awareness as it is is the key to *living in the world but not of it*, to having hourly access to infinity, to witnessing the omnipresent good; the key to experiencing life more abundant, and to unbridled love and relationship.

Freedom of Infinity

Hear this deeply. I did not hear it for twenty years. As it is heard and lived, the freedom of infinity is at hand. All that exists is God (Awareness Itself); and because God is infinite and omnipresent there is no such thing as diluted God, finite God, separate and divided parts of God, temporal God.

Existence is incorporeal, and because the inner is the outer and the outer is the inner, *all* is incorporeal. Incorporeality does not convert itself into a temporal, corporeal life span at the hour of human birth and then return to incorporeality at the hour of death. God is God, Awareness Itself is Awareness Itself, incorporeality is incorporeality. We simply have a corporeal sense of incorporeality, but our sense does not change that which is.

This truth is given us in all the scriptures of the world. It is as clear in Genesis 2:1-5 as in any scripture: "God finished the heavens and the earth, and all the host of them." God (which is spirit and truth, incorporeality) is all of all. An incorporeal existence cannot create (be) corporeal being or form. We are incorporeal beings, not human, not corporeal, not mental, not physical. We and the universe we sense as being corporeal, aren't. All is incorporeal. Herein lies the secret of the infinity of being and of healing that which appears to be discordant, diseased or lacking and limited.

No matter what we believe about life or how we describe it, it is God, the incorporeal. And God is one, omnipresent, invariable, forever the fullness of itself at every point of infinity at the same time; therefore all is that, within and without. Every person, thing, place, condition, activity and amount is the whole of God. A pinhole is the whole of God; a cell is the whole of God; an atom is the whole of God; a subatomic particle (and infinitely beyond) is the whole of God. The infinity (and omnipresence) of the kingdom of heaven and of earth and all the host of them *is* and exists fully manifested and demonstrated *as* all.

The key to having tangible God (the key to the healing consciousness, to witnessing the presence of the infinite, the true harmony, life, joy, abundance, love) is by *our activity* of awareness.[1] Nothing else is involved because nothing other than awareness exists. Hear it deeply. This is the truth that makes us free. Every individual must eventually awaken to this ultimate truth and live by it. Until we do, we continue to suffer. Why not awaken to it now?

This is why the prophet instructs, "Not by might, nor by power, but by my spirit, says the Lord of hosts." (Zechariah 4:6) Every time we are tempted to use mental effort or persuasion, we must stop it. Every time we are tempted to apply physical power to maneuver or manipulate physical things and conditions, we must stop it. By using our minds and physical might, we travel precisely the wrong road. We take our experience away from truth instead of to it.

---

[1] Editor's note: Our activity of awareness is an act of awareness; it is yielding to Awareness Itself as our awareness, as all awareness, as all. It is releasing our attachment to the things, people, circumstances, and conditions (the objects) of awareness and immersing in Awareness Itself. It is a conscious act — a conscious activity, an act of consciousness, an act of awareness.

The key to accessing the freedom of infinity is entirely our activity of *awareness,* not of mental might or physical power. Nothing except the activity of awareness is involved.

As we maintain our awareness in and as Awareness Itself, as we stay detached from the world and its people and things, we are free in awareness, therefore free in experience. But the moment we attach our sense to people, things and conditions, we bind ourselves to finiteness and the pairs of opposites. "Whatsoever ye shall bind on earth shall be bound in heaven". (Matthew 18:18) We lock heaven out of our experience. Our act of awareness is that of belief and attachment to that which appears to be; therefore our experience is finitized and imbued with both good and bad.

A different act of awareness evidences a different experience — not a different human, mind, physical or material act; a different act of *awareness alone* is the key to healing, freedom, and fulfillment. The entire secret to accessing infinity, to the tangible experience of limitlessness, to fulfilled purpose, to true love, true harmony, true peace is to maintain our awareness in and as Awareness Itself, unencumbered by things, by people, by conditions in themselves, yielding to and letting Awareness Itself live us.

Live slightly withdrawn from that which appears to be — restful, relaxed, aware of Awareness Itself. This is the activity of awareness that leads to the gates of infinity.

Let us make it practical.

Start by being aware as you "humanly" would be: aware of and attached to the *objects* of awareness — things, shapes, sizes, sounds, smells, activities; perhaps feeling a worldly pressure, a concern or fear around body or condition; perhaps taking thought for your loved one, family, neighbor or colleague, a deadline at work. Your attention is always on a person, a thing, a place, a circumstance, or on thought itself, and flits from one curiosity to another as this or that lures your attention or reaction.

As humans, we use our awareness to detect, describe and involve ourselves in a complex and variable outer world. We are unwittingly misusing awareness and the objects of awareness. That misuse keeps us imprisoned in the hypnotized state of finiteness and pairs of opposites. Our experience is locked out of earth as it is in heaven.

However, as we awaken to the realization of God, Awareness Itself, being the one omnipresent existence, the finished kingdom of wholeness and fulfillment within and without, we detach from what seems to be and turn to that which is. We cease from attempting to get good from God and wake up to the fact that we already are and have all good embodied in and as our awareness because Awareness is God. Awareness Itself constitutes all that God is and has. We do not get, we do not desire; we *are*. I am that I am. That which I seek I already am.

In this awakened state of awareness we rest and freely behold God "revealing" its image and likeness filling our experience. Actually, God does not reveal anything, God *is*. It is too late for good to be revealed; all is already revealed. The activity of Awareness Itself within spiritualizes us, *opening our eyes to the ever-present good,* and we see clearly.

But what is the practical *way* of it? Let us bring to mind what, to human sense, it appears we need or desire. It might be a need for health, for healing, for money, for love, for companionship. It might be for joy, for a sense of purpose, for happiness, for peace. It might be for harmony, for quiet, stillness, for spiritual attainment. Bring to mind and feel whatever it is in your experience for a minute or two.

(A few minutes in silence)

Now, can you imagine seeking God to give you the room

you are sitting in? God cannot give it to you; you already have it. Bring your most pressing need into awareness again, and realize that the good that seems to be lacking from your experience, as convincingly absent as it appears to be, isn't. In order for any form of good to be absent, God would have to be absent. God is not only present, but is *omnipresence* itself. Where it appears as if a named and defined form of good is absent, all that God is and has is present and fully manifested and demonstrated. Seeking God for that named and defined form of good is like asking God to give you the room you are already sitting in.

Then why can you not *see* the good? Why does it appear as if you do *not* have it? Our Awareness-Itself eyes are closed. We cannot see that which is — just as if our eyes were closed and we could not see the room we are sitting in. Does it matter if we temporarily cannot see it? It is visibly and tangibly right where we are, is it not? All it takes to see it is the opening of our eyes.

God as its infinite formation is ever right where we are. Nothing of fulfillment is absent, invisible, intangible, impractical, or delayed from our immediate apprehension.

While to material sense the good is absent, Awareness Itself sees it clearly and fully. Herein is the secret. The one true faculty of seeing is Awareness Itself seeing itself. Material awareness can never see the forms of Awareness Itself. As we realize that even while our material sense of awareness sees an absence of fulfillment, that which our awareness truly is sees fully-present fulfillment; then as we yield to Awareness Itself, letting it see for us, our eyes are opened and we see clearly.

Our fulfillment has not been manifested or physically drawn to us even though sense may testify to it. *The fulfillment that is always present is now seen.* Awareness Itself, yielded to and given the space and freedom to act in us, seeing itself as it is, is the great secret to the multiplication of fulfillment, to having at hand an infinity of good for any and every sense of need.

> When it was evening, his disciples came to him, and they said to him, This is a lonely place, and it is getting late; dismiss the people so that the men may go to the villages and buy food for themselves. But he said to them, It is not necessary for them to go; you give them something to eat. They said to him, We have nothing here, except five loaves of bread and two fish. Jesus said to them, Bring them here to me. And he ordered the people to sit down on the ground, and he took the five loaves of bread and the two fish, and he looked up to heaven and he blessed them, and he broke them, and gave them to his disciples, and the disciples placed them before the people. So they all ate, and were satisfied; and they took up the fragments which were left over, twelve full baskets. And the men who ate were five thousand, not counting the women and children [probably ten to fifteen thousand people in all].
> (Matthew 14:15-21)

Keeping our sense of awareness in, as and being Awareness Itself *is* the faculty of spiritually seeing and having the infinity of good form.

Live and operate in the world as you normally do, but now do not be *of* it. Living in the world but not of it is our hour-by-hour way of existence. As we go into the world, instead of attaching awareness to particular people, things, colors, amounts, activities and locations, stay pulled back, withdrawn from sense testimony in itself.

You are still in the world, still seeing the objects of sense, but they remain insignificant to you in themselves. You remain unattached to sensory experience in itself. Your awareness abides in the space between you and sensed things, abiding in Awareness Itself. Your focus of attention, your interest, is the love and experience of God. "Love the Lord your God with all your heart, and all your soul, and all your mind, and all your strength." (Mark 12:30) Love the space in between with all your heart, with all your soul, with all your mind, with all your strength. Love Awareness Itself because it is the entirety of God. Be aware of Awareness Itself.

The very instant you realize that you are being aware of Awareness Itself, and are listening, feeling, being attentive to it rather than the *things* of your environment, you are in God consciousness. When you are in God consciousness you have all that God is and has. You can maintain awareness of Awareness Itself even while you are engaged in the world — working, meeting, conversing, shopping, washing the dishes, being with your family or friends. Your awareness is one quarter with them and three quarters in Awareness Itself.

We remain fully functional with the people and circumstances of the world, but we are not *attached* to them. We exist in and as the space between what seems to be us and the things of life. We interact with people, even engage, but not *attach*. This is the secret. We live in and as Awareness Itself which has no things.

The instant you feel detached and the constancy with which you feel it (meaning the greater amount of your awareness, focus, interest and sense is in Awareness Itself), that very instantaneity and constancy are your freedom from "this world." The world can no longer touch you. The world cannot affect you, upset you, hurt you. Disease cannot touch you, and if you have disease, watch how quickly it melts (like ice melting in the sun) as you stay in and live by Awareness Itself. Disease cannot remain in the body of Awareness. Disease is material and requires a material body (belief) to attach to and thrive in. The moment you lift into the true body of Awareness Itself, all physical ailments, even so-called fatal disease, are lost and helpless in and to you. They are rendered impotent and dissipate from experience.

Watch how lack and limitation cannot remain in your experience as you detach from the things of awareness and live as Awareness Itself — knowing that Awareness Itself is infinity and constitutes all that infinity is and has. This instant, as you are aware of Awareness Itself, right here where you stand, you have all that infinity is and has. You have released earth, and "Whatsoever ye release on earth is released in heaven." Not *will* be released, but *is this instant* released in heaven.

And what is the released heaven? It is the visible, tangible, practical form of good. It is the healing; the healing *is* yours here and now; the healthy flesh *is* yours here and now. Why? *Because you are living healthy awareness.* You have lifted from being interested in and concerned for healthy *physical* flesh because you now know that physical experience in itself is false experience. You are interested in what the body truly is, which is healthy awareness. What is healthy awareness? Awareness that is detached from things, people, conditions; awareness that looks up into and seeks the tangible experience of Awareness Itself.

Do you see that the instant you are released from that which appears to be, you have heaven? You have all that God is and has; you are healed, you are whole, you are healthy. You have all the necessary dollars to fulfill every sense of need and opportunity, whether it be a few dollars or a million or a billion. There are no numbers in infinity. The *whole* of infinity is omnipresent. Whether we draw one bucket from the ocean or one million buckets, the ocean instantly fulfills the demand.

It makes no difference to infinity and omnipresence whether twenty hungry people receive food or twenty thousand. There are no multitudes in infinity. Only infinity exists, and only infinity itself can be demonstrated. The

moment infinity itself is demonstrated, it appears as the fulfillment of sense testimony no matter how small or large
that sense of need is. As the ocean fulfills one bucket or one
million, so infinity fulfills one person or one million as the
need appears to be. But the secret is to withdraw all awareness from the sensed need, lift into the infinity of Awareness
Itself, abide *there* feeling the presence, and then beholding
all sense of need fulfilled. But if we remain attached to the
things and conditions of sense, we are not free in Awareness
Itself and cannot experience the infinity of form ever available to us.

Awareness Itself is limitless and unconditional. We have
to be what it is in order to experience its limitlessness objectively. *We have to be limitless and unconditional.* How? By
being aware of and living in and by Awareness Itself.

Healthy flesh is healthy Awareness Itself, and healthy
Awareness Itself is awareness that is unencumbered, unattached to that which seems to be. Prosperous, abundant,
wealthy form is prosperous Awareness Itself — your and my
awareness unencumbered, unattached, free.

Limitlessness of Awareness Itself

Let us prove the limitlessness of Awareness Itself. Become aware of Awareness Itself. Know that it is all that exists. Know that all form is the form of Awareness Itself, not
a form of matter, of location, of definition (even though it
seems to be).

As you feel the presence of Awareness Itself try to find a
limit to it. Try to find its edge, the place where it lacks or is
absent of itself. Try to find a number in it. Try to find an area
of it that lacks the fullness of Awareness Itself. You cannot.
You cannot find any number two to two billion or beyond.
Numbers do not exist. What you find is infinity because

Awareness Itself is infinity itself.

You can prove this in less than a minute. Take your awareness roaming throughout your universe, as far as you wish to roam. Does your awareness run out on you? Do you need to fill it up? Do you need to seek God for more?

When you look up at the moon and the stars, does it use up more awareness than if you're looking at a dollar in your hand or looking at your hand itself or looking at your business or your city? There is no quantity in or about awareness. It takes no more awareness to be aware of a small object vs. large or gargantuan, simple or complex. It takes no more awareness or time to be aware of a single dollar or the entire canopy of heaven with its trillions of stars, its array of planets and its moon. Taking in the breathtaking infinity and beauty of the night sky requires no more seconds than it takes to be aware of a single dollar in our hand.

Awareness is infinite, exhaustless. As we wake up to the truth that all that exists is Awareness Itself, *even as the infinite forms of our "this world" sense,* we have the secret of witnessing the omnipresence, vitality and limitlessness of all form.

Awareness Itself is the only form and is all form. As we are *being* Awareness Itself we are *being* the limitlessness, the truth, the health, the love, the harmony, the infinity, the visibility of all form in our moment-by-moment awareness. However, if we do not know what form is, if we are unaware that form is actually (despite appearance) the infinity and omnipresence of Awareness Itself, then we have finite awareness and therefore finite form. We can *intellectually* realize that Awareness Itself is all, but intellectual awareness is insufficient to *witness* it. We must *live* Awareness Itself. We must live the omnipresence and infinity of Awareness Itself among what appears to be finite form with outlines, locations, size, weight, color, amount. Being the cause of all evidences the effect of the cause we are being.

Awareness and form are one. When, despite appearance, we are being the presence of the boundlessness of Awareness Itself, the boundlessness of form becomes evident. Form is now fueled by the Awareness we are being as it and for it, and therefore reveals itself as the true image and likeness it is, objectively sensed by us.

If we intellectually know that Awareness and form are one, yet have not attained its *practical realization,* we remain unable to evidence it. We see this widely among the world's students. They know the letter of truth, but they are unable to witness it.

The moment a student catches that all is God even though we witness God objectively in what we call the outer; when an individual catches that we have an objective sense of infinity, an objective sense of omnipresence, an objective sense of Awareness Itself, the next thing he or she awakens to is the key to the kingdom of heaven right here as earth: When we are *being* Awareness Itself *as all,* then we are being the truth of form for our experience, and it is quickly evidenced. Then we watch the loaves and fishes multiply, watch dollars multiply, watch health and vitality multiply, watch harmony of mind multiply, watch love multiply, watch peace on earth multiply. In other words, the truth of earth and all it constitutes is evidenced by *our being it.*

"My peace I give unto you, not as the world gives [not material peace, physical peace, human peace, no; *the* peace of Awareness Itself] give I unto you." (John 14:27) It is up to me to give you My Peace when you are in my awareness because I am the only one who can as far I and my experience go. I am the god of my universe, as you are the god of yours. "Ye are gods" (Psalm 82:6; John 10:35) I have to be the god, the cause, unto my universal experience, and you unto yours. I give My Peace — Awareness Itself — unto you, the peace that far exceeds anything human, physical and material yet reveals it-

self as the limitless life, love, happiness, freedom and fulfilled purpose of these.

I am not attempting to bring peace to things and conditions, to humanity or to the world in themselves. *My peace* I
give. The peace, the presence of Awareness Itself, I give as
and to all.

I am the peace of the world, *I am* the light of the world;
I am the life of the world, *I am* the food of the world.

You and I cannot give peace. We do not possess such a
faculty. We are nothing of our own selves. "I of my own self
can do nothing. . . . The Father that dwells in me, he does
the works." (John 5:30; 14:10) Despite what we seem to be and
what education and society have taught us to believe about
ourselves and our capacities, we are the infinity of being.
Our awareness is not human, material and limited; it is
Awareness Itself. As we know this and yield our sense of personal awareness to Awareness Itself, we and our capacity are
infinite — infinity itself. In this state of awareness we simply
behold the infinity of all reveal itself in front of us and as
whatever we do because we are *being what infinity is* as person, body, thing, condition, amount, business, and world.
My peace, *my* infinity, *my* life, *my* love give I unto you.

It is my work to feed the world with Awareness Itself. "I
must be about my Father's business. . . . Feed my sheep." (Luke
2:49; John 21:16-17) I have to be the god of my world: I have to
feed the world with the light, the spirit, the truth; feed the
world with Awareness Itself. How? By *being* Awareness Itself
as and for all.

Now watch how the Father within you does the works.
The Father within you, Awareness Itself, sees itself as you
and for you, and there right where you are (wherever that is
and whatever the condition seems to be) is the miracle of
truth — healing, prosperity, abundance, wealth, love and
harmony — made evident, real, visible and tangible.

Be the Wealth of the World

We have to be the wealth of the world. What is wealth? What appears to sense as tangible visible wealth is our wealth of awareness of Awareness Itself. Poverty in any shape or form, including a lack of money or business success, is our poverty of awareness of Awareness Itself. "If you do not know yourselves, you dwell in poverty and it is you who are that poverty." (The Gospel of Thomas, Saying 3) This is a hard saying the first time we hear it. When it is understood, it is instant freedom

If anything seems amiss in our lives, if anything seems to be lacking or limited, if our or our friend's body is sick or injured, if anything is discordant or aversive, it is our lack of awareness of Awareness Itself appearing to be the outer problem.

Let us become wealthy in Awareness Itself. Let us become wealthy in God consciousness, wealthy in God. Let us keep our minds on God, have no false idols, have no other gods except Me. "Turn ye not unto idols, nor make to yourselves molten gods: I am [Awareness Itself is] the Lord your God. . . . Thou shalt have none other gods before me." (Leviticus 19:14; Deuteronomy 5:7)

Do not be hoodwinked into believing that anything of sense testimony is an entity unto itself. Only Awareness Itself is entity. All "else" is imagery of sense — images either clearly seen or clouded by belief. If we live by belief we suffer. As we live by Awareness Itself we are free.

Never believe that *I* am absent, or that *I* am discordant. *I* am you, and *I* am everything of your field of awareness, unto infinity. You have never been required to live life yourself, to create success, to find and keep love, to be free and fulfilled. *I* am you, and *I* am that of you which reveals myself as the fulfillment of all you are, all you have, and all you experience.

"I am the Lord, and there is none else, there is no God be-side me." (Isaiah 45:5) The kingdom of God is inside you and it is outside you. If we believe there is anything amiss in our world, in our body, in our minds; if we believe anything is lacking, limited; if we believe any form, amount or quality of good is absent anywhere in our kingdom, then we have not yet awakened to the fact that God — Awareness Itself — is our God, our fulfillment of being and purpose, perfectly real, visible and tangible within and without at every moment.

As we become wealthy in God, we become wealthy in good, no matter what we name that good, and God, in the language of this book, is Awareness Itself. We become wealthy in, we become interested in, we seek nothing but, we adventure in Awareness Itself; and because Awareness Itself constitutes all that God is and has (infinity and om-nipresence within and without), we quickly discover that as we become wealthy in Awareness Itself, we have all the earth's good ever at hand — boundless, ever-present good right where we are.

Live As and In and For Awareness Itself

Live as and in and for Awareness Itself. Keep your senses slightly pulled back from that which seems to be so that you have the spaciousness to hear God, to feel God, to feel the presence of Awareness Itself — to live it and breathe it. *I live and move and have my being in and as Awareness Itself, and Awareness Itself lives and moves and has its being in and as me.*

Then in that spaciousness, in that released earth, you *feel* the presence; and as you feel the presence, you are and have all the good of the infinite. The feeling is the visibility, is the very form, is the very presence of your good. Nothing else has to happen because nothing else exists. This is why we must stay released from everything else. The more detached and released we stay, the more of Awareness Itself is evident as the abundant good of our health, of our relationships, and of our world.

The more detached and released we remain in Awareness Itself, the more Awareness Itself sees itself as and for us, and performs as us and for us. Then that which seemed to be an unyielding lack or limitation or discord quickly melts like a cube of ice in the hot midday sun, revealing itself as true image and likeness — earth as it is in heaven.

We will probably not be able to maintain a complete detachment and release, but we do not have to. Sincerity is what matters. When we sincerely give it the best we can hour by hour, our effort is always enough. It is not the number of hours we manage to stay in truth but the depth of our sincerity.

It is an act of awareness, not ever an act of mentality, physicality or materiality. Earth is heaven, heaven is earth, but we have been hypnotized by belief and have therefore been unaware of truth. Put belief aside — nothing need be done with belief. Lift right into Awareness Itself this minute. Do you see how all it takes — the great secret — is our act of awareness? Our act of awareness takes us from our *sense* into Awareness Itself. Here we rest, yield, and witness the activity of Awareness Itself being all. This one act opens our eyes from unawareness into awareness.

As Awareness Itself, we revere and adore God with all our hearts, all our souls, all our minds, and all our strength. We revere and adore Awareness Itself. We do not revere and adore the things in and of themselves: the people, the conditions, the wealth. We revere and adore God because God is the only. God is the truth of our lives, *the one* life, the *one* existence, the *one* reality.

I discovered this when I was experiencing a long period of great pain and suffering. One day it got so bad that I was beside myself. I didn't know what to do. I'd read all the books, I'd listened to all the classes, I'd done all the meditating and sitting in the silence I could do, yet all that was happening was a worsening of the cancer to the point where it was finishing me. So I did not know what to do. I was overwhelmed and felt helpless. What more? There was nothing more I could do. It was as if God was ignoring me. The condition and the pain kept getting worse.

Finally, driven into the corner, out of ideas and hope, I decided to trust truth. I decided that the one thing I could still do that I hadn't done is truly trust that when I keep my mind on God, and when I empty myself of self and truly give myself to God, I will experience God. When I *really do* love God with all my heart and all my soul and all my mind and all my strength, I will experience God because as I keep my consciousness filled with God, as I keep my attention on and trust in Awareness Itself, then, because Awareness Itself is and constitutes all that God is, I will find myself full of God.[1]

That particular day I decided I have nothing left but that. Of course, I am sure I read this on the first page of the first truth book I ever had. But now it was time to actually do it. Well, a miracle happened. I discovered that within just five or ten or fifteen minutes of keeping my mind on God, keeping my awareness on Awareness Itself, all the pain dissolved. That was a major "result" for me because the pain was excruciating. It all dissolved.

The next thing I realized was that the more I kept my mind on Awareness Itself and the more I truly trusted Awareness Itself as being my real and present help, the more I forgot about the cancer, and the more pain-free was my

---

[1] Editor's note: Although Paul did not have the term "Act of Awareness" at the time, that is exactly what was taking place in him.

experience. The next thing I realized was that I didn't have cancer. It disappeared. No scars, no signs, nothing. Well, it was a revelation that changed the course of my life forever. Awareness Itself truly is all that exists.

Discipline

When we bring through the discipline to keep our awareness on and in and as Awareness Itself, we infallibly discover that the miracle of truth becomes evident throughout our minds, bodies and worlds. It is infallible because Awareness Itself *is* individual being and individual world. All it takes is the transformation of awareness from our personal sense of awareness to Awareness Itself.

Bring forth that discipline. Learn to be in the world but not of it. Practice the presence of God in this very way. You can start right now. Nothing is stopping us from experiencing truth inside us and outside us except our lack of discipline to keep our awareness in Awareness Itself.

If we experience a delay in the evidence of truth, it is a delay in *our activity* of awareness (as I unwittingly delayed it for twenty years). The sense of delay is only this. There is no actual delay because truth already is. Problems can seem to be stubbornly stuck, unyielding, but it is really *our* unyielding belief in and attachment to that which seems to be, outpicturing itself as an unyielding problem. It isn't that because all is Awareness Itself. Our lack of discipline in staying aware of Awareness Itself is the only problem.

Staying in Awareness Itself we live in the world but not of it. Rest, rest, rest. Devote yourself to God, to truth. Rest in Awareness Itself. Give yourself the greatest gift in heaven and earth: periods throughout the day where you are truly lifted in and rested in Awareness Itself, simply listening, feeling, beholding. This is devotion to Awareness Itself.

Sit down, or lie down (whatever feels best to you) and devote this hour to God. Just be silent, be still, and know that Awareness Itself is God. Let God get on with being God as God as you and as your world.

Then, when this period feels "complete" to you, get up and be in the world but not of it. Never again be of the world because by being of the world, you are blinded, unable to see truth. But being in the world but not of it is the very faculty of open eyes, open ears, of seeing clearly, of witnessing the presence of the infinite. As we feel the presence happening within, that is Awareness Itself seeing Itself as and for us. I live yet not I, Awareness Itself lives me.

(A few minutes of silence)

You are whole. You now have every good that God is and has, and you see it as you stay in Awareness Itself. You will see it everywhere: more flowers, color, fragrance and joy in your world than you have ever before noticed; more birds and bird song in your world than you have ever before noticed; more love filling you and your relationship than you have ever before experienced. You will notice new vitality, strength, energy, youthfulness in the body that you have never before experienced. You will have friendship, companionship, abundance; doors will open everywhere you go, and understanding, support, supply and resource will stand at your door and knock.

Peace will be yours to an extent you never dreamed possible. You will see and meet happy, loving, giving people; and you will watch as people standing in line and at checkouts who seem to be unhappy, sad, or ill spring into happiness, life, and joy in your silent presence.

You will witness miracles, and you will witness the miraculous in the clothes of normality and what appears to be wondrous coincidence. You will find the treasures of heaven everywhere you go because they *are* everywhere you go. You will experience earth as it is in heaven presenting herself to you as a daily gift of love. You never have to go looking for her. She presents herself to you.

It is the Father's good pleasure to give you the kingdom.

Visit www.miracleself.com/MSBooksOnline.html
to freely read unabridged Miracle Self books
(no email, password or fee is required)

———————————

The Miracle Self Monthly Letter is available free
upon request.

Go to www.miracleself.com for free subscription

Printed in Great Britain
by Amazon

41638593R00087